You Can't
Spank a Kid
in a Snowsuit
*and other lessons
on parenting*

You Can't Spank a Kid in a Snowsuit

& Other Lessons on Parenting

BRUCE HOWARD

Tyndale House Publishers, Inc.
Wheaton, Illinois

Dedication

With love and thanksgiving to my parents, who have been the ones to introduce me to their Father. In doing so, they have shown me the way to lead my own children. It is because of their love, instruction, nurturing, and example that grandparent, parent, and grandchild are all now brother and sister in Christ.

Copyright © 1994 by Bruce Howard
All rights reserved

Cover illustration copyright © 1994 by Rick Kirkman

Unless otherwise noted, Scripture quotations are taken from the *New American Standard Bible,* © 1960, 1962, 1963, 1968, 1971, 1972, 1973, 1975, 1977 by The Lockman Foundation. Used by permission.

Scripture verses marked TLB are taken from *The Living Bible,* copyright © 1971 owned by assignment by KNT Charitable Trust. All rights reserved.

Library of Congress Cataloging-in-Publication Data

Howard, Bruce,   date
    You can't spank a kid in a snowsuit, and other lessons from
parenting / Bruce Howard.
        p. cm.
    ISBN 0-8423-1334-6
    1. Child rearing—Religious aspects—Christianity.   2. Parenting—
Religious aspects—Christianity.   I. Title.
HQ769.3.H695   1994
649'.1—dc20   94-6420

Printed in the United States of America

99 98 97 96 95 94
 7   6   5   4   3   2

CONTENTS

PART ONE

Lessons about Parenting

CHAPTER 1

You Can't Spank a Kid in a Snowsuit

There are as many theories on the merits and evils of spanking as there are parents, but I believe there is nothing like a good spanking to get your point across with a child. I was the recipient of my share of spankings, and I firmly believe I'm a better man for having received them.

Spankings in my family were administered most often by my mother. Mom worked at home, so she usually happened to be the parent closest at hand when a spanking was deserved. She had a thin little belt that she would use. It would even fit in her purse, and she could bring it to church. All she had to do was rattle that purse a little bit and my brothers and I would shape up real quick.

If Mom gave me the *most* spankings, Dad gave me the *best*—or *worst*, depending on how you look at it. Once Dad and I were playing a game of Ping-Pong. I was a terrible player, and my Dad was quite good, but somehow it didn't make sense to me that he should win. I was an extremely competitive child, which is just a polite way of saying that I was a sore loser. I remember being particularly obnoxious one afternoon. I was carrying on because I was losing in spite of my dad's best efforts at helping me beat him, short of an outright forfeit. It wasn't enough that my father had taken time out and condescended to play with a beginner like me; I had to win as well. Dad tolerated my behavior only so long, and then I crossed the line.

The next serve my father made with that Ping-Pong paddle was to my backside. He may well have served up twenty-one winners in a row right on my backcourt, and I didn't sit down for a long time. What's more important, it was a much longer time before I smarted off to my dad and behaved in that manner again.

Spanking is not the only way to sanction a child. We have found that sometimes, taking away privileges is an effective way to get a point across and to teach a lesson. Regardless of what punishment is used, the whole endeavor of punishing children in order to bring about morally correct behavior is a difficult thing to figure out. Selecting and administering the appropriate type and degree of punishment to match an offense is not easy. I recall one particular instance where I didn't get it right.

It had been a terrific winter's afternoon. The snow in the yard was deep and sticky white. I had been having a wonderful time building snowmen and playing with my two sons and my daughter in this winter wonderland.

How is it that great times like that have to be spoiled by misbehavior? As so often happens with kids, one gets to teasing another, and one of the boys took it upon himself to see to it that his sister spent an inordinate amount of time in the snow. When I wasn't looking, he would push her down—not hard or maliciously, just insidiously.

It may have started off in fun, but it certainly did not end up that way. My daughter informed me that her brother was pushing her down in the snow. It was not immediately clear to me that this was a problem, because up until this point, the three kids had been laughing. If my daughter had been getting pushed into the snow, she must have thought it was fun, judging by her laughter. But I accepted her complaint and issued a cease and desist order to the offending brother. When I saw the brother on the verge of repeating his offense, I intervened and promised serious consequences if he carried out his intentions. In response to this intervention, the boy hesitated—and then gave his sister one last good push into the snow.

This was nothing short of open rebellion. I saw red and instantly moved to follow through on my end of the bargain. The only thing I didn't take into account was the fact that the boy was wearing a snowsuit. The moment I picked him up, I realized you can't spank a kid in a snowsuit. I thought about taking him inside to spank him, but it generally took me a half an hour with a blowtorch to extract a kid from a snowsuit, and I felt the situation needed a more immediate response.

So what *do* you do with a kid in a snowsuit? I had picked this boy up and was holding him suspended in the air. All I could do was tromp around the yard, holding this kid in the air, trying to figure out what to do next. My son didn't know if I had flipped out and was playing some new kind of game or if he was about to breathe his last.

I was so frustrated and angry that in the end, all I could think of doing was dropping him in an evergreen hedge in the corner of the yard. I just walked up to the bush and shoved him right down in the center of it.

"Don't you *dare* move!"

It was a needless warning. There was no way he could *possibly* move. Unless I decided to later extricate him, he would be stuck there at least until spring.

My son reacted immediately with a wail that would scare a spook. As angry as I was, I was still surprised by the intensity of his cry. Getting dumped in a bush was not a common punishment, but it couldn't be as bad as a spanking. And yet, he had never cried like this when getting a spanking. I soon discovered the reason for his crying: one of the sticks in the bush had penetrated his snowsuit and scraped his back. The abrasion was very painful and left a noticeable mark.

I believe that was one of my most frustrating fathering experiences. My son had demonstrated willful rebellion and deserved swift and just punishment. Unfortunately, the punishment, though swift, was not just. You don't scrape a child's back with a sharp stick as a means of punishment. But that's what happened when I shoved him feet-first into the bush. And it was all because I couldn't spank him in a snowsuit.

As soon as I understood what had happened, I grabbed my son and took him inside. We managed to get the snowsuit off and attend to the wound.

When the pain, both physical and emotional, had subsided, we talked. My son and I talked about the actions and motivations that had precipitated all of this. He was truly repentant. So was I. I was able to explain to him why I did what I did. I also admitted my limitations as a father and that in trying to do what is right, I would sometimes make mistakes. There was no mistake in deciding that a punishment was deserved. The mistake came in that the punishment was not appropriate.

In the last analysis, there were lots of tears but even more hugs, and we all learned our lesson.

And He will judge the world in righteousness; He will execute judgment for the peoples with equity. (Ps. 9:8)

My son, do not regard lightly the discipline of the Lord, nor faint when you are reproved by Him; For those whom the Lord loves He disciplines, and He scourges every son whom He receives. (Heb. 12:5-6)

Furthermore, we had earthly fathers to discipline us, and we respected them; shall we not much rather be subject to the Father of spirits, and live? For they disciplined us for a short time as seemed best to them, but He disciplines us for our good, that we may share His holiness. (Heb. 12:9-10)

For the Lord will not reject forever, for if He causes grief, then He will have compassion according to his abundant lovingkindness. For He does not afflict willingly, or grieve the sons of men. (Lam. 3:31-33)

He will not always strive with us; nor will He keep His anger forever. (Ps. 103:9)

These verses provide insight into how the heavenly Father deals with the problem of punishing his children. They offer us at least three principles to remember in disciplining our own children.

When God disciplines, the punishment is fair. God judges in

7

righteousness, and he is always equitable. But I don't have the wisdom of God, and I am susceptible to errors in judgment. I have found it helpful to consult with my wife in assessing the fairness of a punishment. She may be less emotionally involved in a particular situation and can be more objective. As the children have grown older, we have sometimes been able to ask *them* to help us with assessing the fairness of a punishment. If they think we are being unduly harsh, we will try to listen to their reasons.

When God disciplines, the punishment is formative. Punishment is not meant to beat a person down. It should build up character. Punishment should help us become better people. This is God's intent for us, and it should be our intent for our children.

When God disciplines, the punishment is final. God doesn't nurse a grudge. I can and sometimes do. If I have been angry with a child, I can let that child feel my displeasure for hours. The tendency to revisit past offenses is destructive in any relationship. God doesn't do it with us, and we shouldn't do it with our children. Once punishment is administered, we have to decide to move ahead with life.

The next time you are in a position to administer discipline, I suggest you ask yourself these three questions: Is it fair? Is it formative? Will it be final?

If the answer is yes, then go ahead. If not, try talking it through with your spouse. You may even want to talk it through with your child. Finally, consider asking the heavenly Father. He's been there plenty of times.

CHAPTER 2

Mothers to the Rescue

If you ever have a couple of hours to kill and are looking for some cheap entertainment, I highly recommend going to a park and watching a game called T-ball. This is baseball for kids just out of diapers.

No one ever told me T-ball was an optional activity for families. I thought it was a requirement for living within our city limits, just like paying property taxes. So when the time came, I dutifully signed my son up for T-ball.

I grew up playing sandlot baseball, so I thought I understood the game. But I must admit I was a bit bewildered when, as a T-ball parent, I received a sheet of paper with the rules of the game on one side and the after-game treat assignments on the other. The game wasn't measured in innings; it was measured in hours. A side would be retired after three outs or fifteen runs, whichever came first.

I later learned the reason for the notorious fifteen-run rule. It is virtually impossible to get someone *out* in T-ball. To do so, a kid in the field has to either catch the ball on the fly or pick it up and throw it to first base before the batter gets there. Even if the kid could remember what he or she was supposed to do, there is the matter of execution. Execution was very problematic. The end result is that there are few outs ever made in T-ball. Typical game scores are something like 79 to 65.

My son regularly defied the laws of T-ball probability. He would make outs. This was because, being left-handed, he'd hit the ball to first base. But it was also due to the fact that for some reason, he wouldn't run after he hit the ball. He would stand at home plate, basking in the glory and satisfaction of having made contact with the ball. Then—if the Spirit moved—he *might* head on down to first base. But he would never run. He would prance. That's right; he would *prance*. He would spring, one step at a time, carving imaginary arcs through the air with each leap. Even in T-ball it's hard to get a run this way.

The fact that my boy would regularly make outs bothered me for the first couple of games. But my attitude soon changed, because my boy didn't care in the least if he made it to first safely or not. If he didn't care, why should I? Besides, I—and other parents, as well—grew to see my son as something of a hero because his making outs speeded up the game. Everyone appreciated that!

I was somewhat intrigued by the fact that my son would not run. At home I would watch him, and it was always the same. He would prance, but he would not run. Prancing suited him just fine. So I reconciled myself to the fact that my boy would never be a track star. It was of no real concern to me because I believed there were many more important things in life than athletic prowess.

The spring T-ball season ended, summer came, and, with summer, the Fourth of July. For our family, this holiday has

always meant a gathering of the clan at my parents' home.
My kids love this day for many reasons, but one of the main
ones is that they get to be with all of the cousins. There is a
mess of cousins in our family. On this particular afternoon,
most of the aunts and uncles were out on the porch talking
and keeping half an eye on the small herd of children whirl-
ing about like a dust devil in the front yard.

I remember observing a pack of wagons, tricycles, scoot-
ers, and kids making its way down the sidewalk. The pack
progressed to the end of the block and disappeared around
the corner. Nobody was worried, but I paid a bit closer attention waiting for the pack to reappear and head back in our
direction. After some time, they came back around the corner, but I could tell instantly that something was wrong.
Even from that distance I could hear shouts and screams.

At the head of the pack, one kid was running, quickly out-
distancing the others. I remarked to a brother standing next
to me, "Look at that kid run! That kid is *fast!*"

You can imagine my surprise when I realized this was my
own son, the prancer. I thought, *This can't be,* but it was. I
soon learned the reason for my son's behavior. Not too far
behind him was an irate little wiener of a dog, yapping in a
most threatening way.

"That dog is after my boy," I said.

The other uncles all agreed, and what did we do? We
stood there. We all kind of wanted to see if he could outrun
this little wiener dog, and so all the men just stood there and
watched.

This incident perfectly illustrates why God invented
mothers. A mother would never just stand there and let a
dog chase her child, even if it *were* only a wiener dog! And
that goes double for grandmothers. When my mother saw
what was happening, she instantly took action. She grabbed

the nearest weapon she could find, which happened to be a cloth diaper that one of the babies was using for a security blanket. And so, armed with a diaper, the matriarch of our family took off after that little wiener dog in a way that would cause a Great Dane to tremble. My son was saved.

After the excitement had subsided, I had a chance to reflect on how that same woman had come to *my* rescue many years earlier. I grew up in an era when it was fashionable to have plastic pink flamingos in your front yard, and a typical neighborhood prank would consist of gathering as many flamingos as you could find and sticking them in front of somebody's house. On one occasion, our flamingos had been snatched, and I was sure I knew who had done it. It was Dick Dunk. He was a bit of a neighborhood bully, and in the past, he had often bragged of similar exploits. When I confronted him with my accusation, he hotly denied it. I, however, persisted with my accusations, and that, as it turned out, was not a smart thing to do. Dick Dunk was a foot taller and three years older than I. I managed to provoke him to the point where he completely lost his temper. At that point he grabbed me by the back of my hair, dragged me around the side of the house, turned on the water spigot, and proceeded to bang the back of my head repeatedly against the spout. This was a wet and painful experience.

My mother heard my cries and appeared, armed that time with a broom. I still vividly remember (with, I confess, a certain amount of pleasure) watching her chase Dick Dunk down the street, vigorously applying that broom to Dick's where-the-sun-don't-shine.

Thank God for mothers.

It wasn't long after the wiener dog incident that I came across the following passage of Scripture:

> In the days of Shamgar the son of Anath, in the days
> of Jael, the highways were deserted, and travelers went
> by roundabout ways. The peasantry ceased, they
> ceased in Israel, until I, Deborah, arose, until I arose,
> a mother in Israel. (Judg. 5:6-7)

Deborah was a woman who rose to the pinnacle of
political power by common consent of the people. She
served as a judge for the people of Israel. She used to
hold court under the "palm tree of Deborah," somewhere
between Ramah and Bethel. The times were very difficult
for her people. They lived in political and economic bond-
age to the Canaanites. All economic activity had virtually
ceased, and the people were living at a subsistence level.
It was the maternal instinct in Deborah that initiated a
series of events that culminated with God's intervention
on behalf of the Israelites.

The men were not able to figure out what ought to be
done. It took a woman like Deborah to get things going in
the right direction. Her legacy to her people was an entire
generation of peace.

The example of Deborah and my own experience have
taught me something about raising children. God's plan was
for children to be raised by both mothers *and* fathers. Sometimes my instinct as a father is wrong. The wiener dog incident in our family was a good example: the men did the
wrong thing, and the mother, acting on instinct, did just
what was needed.

I have seen that when it comes to raising our children, my
wife and I will often come to an issue with different perspectives. I am growing to appreciate this more as time goes by. I
don't believe having different perspectives implies that we
can't reach a common conclusion regarding a problem. On

13

the contrary, thoughtful communication and respect for each other's ideas will usually draw us to a better conclusion than either could reach alone.

I grew up watching "Father Knows Best." It was a delightful show, but the title is flawed. Fathers should by all means exercise leadership in the home, but sound leadership will always heed wise counsel. The wisest of dads should recognize that sometimes "mother knows best." I know a little would-be wiener-dog victim who would agree.

CHAPTER 3

And What Are Great Running Backs Made of? Would You Believe Sugar and Spice and Everything Nice?

Of all the sporting events that I have either witnessed or participated in, my little girl's first touchdown run will, for me, be the highlight of all time.

Our family has been blessed with two boys and one girl. Our daughter is the youngest. As a father, I have always found it easier to play with the guys. I instinctively know what to do when the guys want me to play with them. My daughter's interests in playing are often very different.

Lisa likes to play Smooshees, and through practice I too have become quite good at it. Smooshees are soft little animallike creatures that can be compressed ("smooshed," if you will) and stuffed into little plastic houses, swings, chairs, and other accessories that come with Smooshees dolls. I am also good at playing restaurant and school, which seem to be favorite playtime activities for Lisa. Though I must confess that whenever we play school, I wind up getting sent to the principal's office.

Even though Lisa has consistently shown interest in activities apart from those her brothers pursue, she will often enthusiastically enter into playing with the boys, their friends, and dear old Dad.

This was the case the day Lisa decided to join us in a Saturday afternoon pickup game of football. I took Lisa on my team, and together we decided to *take on the boys!* It was going to be Lisa and me against four boys—her two brothers and two of their friends. Lisa was seven years old, and the boys' ages ranged from nine to eleven. I'd say Lisa and I were in slightly over our heads, but hey, it was just for fun, right?

Not on your life! This was serious business for these guys. To let Dad beat them was bad enough. But to get beat by Dad and your little sister, well, that would be just a bit more than any nine-, ten-, or eleven-year-old boy could take.

The game commenced and, surprisingly, Lisa and I were holding our own. This was due primarily to sloppy execution on the part of our opponents. The pressure of having to beat your little sister was really getting to them—they couldn't seem to do anything right. The entire game was a low-scoring, defensive struggle.

Lisa didn't really understand the game. It was hard for her to throw the ball, and she couldn't seem to remember which way to run for a touchdown. Consequently, we had trouble scoring points. Defense came easier for her. All I had to do was tell her to chase the boy with the ball, grab him, and hang on to him until I got there. That was no problem. She could play defense like a pit bull.

The game progressed nicely from my perspective, and it came down to the ten-minutes-to-supper warning. Time for just one last series of downs. Lisa and I had the ball. This was it; all tied up and our chance to be heroes. In our Daddy-daughter huddle of two, I put my hands on her little shoulders and asked her, "Lisa, do you want to beat the boys?"

Lisa hadn't consistently run in the right direction all afternoon. She had dropped every pass I had thrown her way. But in response to my question, her blue eyes sparkled like fireworks on the Fourth of July. I needed no other reply.

"Listen, honey, this is what you do. Hike the ball to me when I say *two*. Then I want you to take three steps forward, stop, turn around, and catch the ball when I throw it to you. *Don't drop the ball,* because if you do, then we won't beat the boys. After you catch the ball, run as fast as you can to the apple tree. I'll take care of the boys."

It wasn't much of a plan. But whatever was lacking in strategy was more than made up for in hope. Lisa bounced up to the line of scrimmage, snapped the ball, ran her short route, and—to the surprise of everyone—turned around and caught the ball! It was the first reception of her career. It was the first of her entire life. Four shaken little boys then moved to descend on her like a pack of wolf cubs. I headed them off and gave the first of the boys a good-natured little push. With just the one little push I saw four boys bite the dust like dominoes. I flopped down on the pile and grabbed the whole pack in a bear hug. They reacted instantly with cries of foul play and desperately squirmed to free themselves from my grasp.

I looked up from the pile to see Lisa running for all she was worth . . . in the wrong direction. I screamed, *"To the apple tree—run to the apple tree!!"*

She heeded the warning and turned to recover lost

ground. I was fast losing my grip on the boys, and some of the pack escaped. The chase was on. Lisa cut sharply to the right and doubled back around the wood pile. She climbed over the pile and skirted around the shed. She broke into the open, only to find herself facing an angry and desperate defender. No worries. She darted for cover in the lilac bush. From there she crawled through the hedge to the safety of the neighbor's yard, ran up the parallel field, and reappeared in our yard just a few feet from the apple tree, the official end zone. She crossed the goal line, spiked the ball like the best of them, and began celebrating the victory.

I had watched most of this from ground level. But when Lisa scored, I jumped up and ran to join the celebration. There were high fives, low fives, behind-your-back fives, and cheering to beat the band. For the guys, it was a different story. They stood there with sullen, angry looks and fire in their bellies.

"It's not fair!"

"You pushed us!"

"You held us!"

"You tripped me!"

"Yeah, and she ran out of bounds!"

I good-naturedly replied, "There's nothing at all unfair. I made one little block. I didn't hold you, I merely decided to lay down and catch my breath. I can't help it if you can't stand on your own two feet without tripping, and no one ever said you couldn't use the neighbor's yard."

The wolf pack was dumbfounded at this mockery of justice. There were cries for appeal, but there was no higher court. Father had spoken. The touchdown was upheld, and together, Daddy and daughter had beaten the boys.

After the game, I had a little bit of relationship mending to take care of. My sons felt betrayed by my actions and by my final ruling in favor of Lisa's touchdown. Their feelings, you may agree, were probably not entirely unjustified. After things cooled off a bit, I sat the guys down and explained that in football, they had different abilities than Lisa had. I tried to explain that I felt Lisa needed some special encouragement and that we should be willing to make some allowances for her being new to the game and for being younger.

To be honest, I'm not sure they understood. But as a kindness to their little sister, they agreed to accept the outcome— as long as we didn't rub it in. That sounded fair enough to me, so we let it go.

It occurred to me later that people often measure justice in the same way that my boys did. *Fairness* is often defined as making sure everyone gets identical treatment. Consideration offered to one and not to another is deemed as being unfair.

Allowing Lisa to run way out of bounds, in addition to my greatly restricting the boys' ability to pursue their own interests (chasing Lisa), struck them as being most unfair. But as the father of both Lisa and the boys, I felt it was in the best interest of our family to allow Lisa to accomplish something that she had never done before. It was a great boost for her, and it really cost the boys nothing except a little pride. OK . . . maybe a *lot* of pride. But learning to swallow your pride isn't always a bad lesson in itself. Especially when doing so really gives someone else a lift.

To be sure, sometimes justice will be served by treating everyone in exactly the same way. But then there are other times when perfectly egalitarian treatment will not be fair. In football, nine- and eleven-year-old boys have distinct advantages over seven-year-old girls. It was very reasonable to have different standards for the kids in order to make it a *fair* game.

Telling this to my sons was much easier than having to accept the same lesson from my heavenly Father. Sometimes, being fair just means that God must treat us all the same way. But it is also reasonable to expect times when he has a special plan for a certain person that may call for individualized and unique attention.

> Again I looked throughout the earth and saw that the swiftest person does not always win the race, nor the strongest man the battle, and that wise men are often poor, and skillful men are not necessarily famous. . . . Here is my final conclusion: fear God and obey his commandments, for this is the entire duty of man. For God will judge us for everything we do, including every hidden thing, good or bad. (Eccles. 9:11; 12:13-14, TLB)

The circumstances of life will be different for every person. This strikes us as unfair. We don't always like it when life deals us a heavy blow while another person enjoys a seemingly unwarranted blessing from the hand of God. Instead of getting angry at God, we would do well to trust him to know what is best and just for each of us and all of us.

By the way, if you're ever playing football and need a running back, I know where you can find one. She's cute, cagey, and has blue eyes. Best of all, she loves to beat the boys!

CHAPTER 4

How Come Daddy Has a Vise-Grip on His Ear?

I must confess that I cannot, with any degree of confidence, tell you what word was the first to come out of my daughter's mouth. I simply can't remember. It was probably something like *ma-ma* or *da-da*. I am pretty certain, however, that the first complete sentence she uttered has to have been: "Daddy, can I get my ears pierced?"

Lisa was campaigning for this before she could walk. In retrospect, I am convinced it was a conspiracy. My wife, of course, was in on the plot. Even the aunts, the uncles, and the cousins were all against me on this issue. But I knew for sure that I was going to lose this one when my father-in-law bought Lisa a pair of Minnie Mouse pierced earrings from Walt Disney World. (And to think, this was the same man who had years earlier told my wife: "If God wanted holes in your ears he would have made them that way!")

When I saw those earrings, I knew it was only a matter of

time. I had to buy time. But how? I opted for the age-old, arbitrary paternal mandate.

"Not until she is twenty-one!"

That one went up in smoke.

"No daughter of mine is getting her ears pierced before she is sixteen years old!"

I crashed and burned on that.

"Twelve years old, and *that's final!!*"

I must have sounded more convincing than I felt, because after my twelve-years-of-age edict, the pressure subsided somewhat. I held out for several years, and there was a time when I actually thought we might make it to twelve. But then Ruthie, my wife, did something totally unfair. She sat me down and asked me very simply to explain *why* I believed that Lisa should wait until she was twelve to have her ears pierced. What was so important about being twelve? Was it arbitrary, or did I have good reasons?

Alas, I was found out. I had no good reasons. It was arbitrary. I was speechless.

Even though I couldn't articulate any decent sort of response, I knew that there had to be one. For I felt it deep within as strongly as I felt anything. All my instincts as a father told me that we had to go slow on the pierced ears. Ruthie must have seen this in my face because she didn't press the matter. She truly wanted to understand my position but couldn't unless I helped her. I told her I'd think about it and try again later to express my reasons.

It took some time to analyze why I felt the way I did. In the end, I was able to focus on the root of my concerns. I didn't want my children buying into the idea that their worth as a person depended on how others reacted to their appearance.

Physical appearance can be so fleeting. It has nothing to

do with the ultimate worth of a person. But our culture seems to hold physical beauty up as one of the most important measures of a human being's value. So it bothered me that my daughter was so concerned about wearing pierced earrings to look good.

Ruthie understood, and even shared my concern, but she also suggested that some little girls liked to wear earrings simply for the fun of it. Having a collection of earrings could be just like having a collection of baseball cards.

I had to admit that I never had thought of it in those terms before. So Ruthie and I settled on a strategy that would accommodate my concern and yet make some sense to Lisa. I sat down with Lisa and explained to her why I was worried about earrings. I talked to her about outer beauty and inner beauty. I told her how pretty I thought she was on the outside. I also explained to her that inner beauty takes a lot more time. It's not nearly as easy as putting on a pair of earrings to make sure that people are pretty on the inside. I told her we would wait and watch to see how she was growing in inner beauty. When she was as pretty on the inside as she was on the outside, then she could get her ears pierced. It was like waiting and watching for a flower to bloom. We were sure that it would, but it just would take some time.

The flower bloomed in the spring of her third-grade year. It wasn't dramatic. It was just a growing confidence that Ruthie and I developed in our daughter's values and choices. I became convinced that for Lisa, collecting and wearing earrings *was* much the same as my boys collecting baseball cards. Society also places undue value on athletic prowess, but collecting baseball cards isn't going to ruin a kid. Earrings weren't going to ruin Lisa.

I was surprised by how much fun I had when I bought her a pair. It took me quite some time to pick them out, but I was pleased with them. She was sitting at the kitchen table when Ruthie and I gave them to her. One look in those eyes made it all worthwhile. Lisa understood immediately that the gift of earrings represented permission for getting her ears pierced. To say this made her happy would be to say the Chicago Cubs were pleased to win a pennant. She was elated! But I also believe she was very gratified to receive confirmation from Mom and Dad that we were pleased with her progress at developing an inner beauty.

Only time will tell whether I have been right or wrong in all of this. But I was encouraged when, right after Lisa had her ears pierced, she said to me, "Don't worry, Daddy. I'll always try to be as pretty on the inside as I am on the outside."

A few days after this event I thought a little bit of fun might be in order. I got ahold of a pair of fake diamond-stud earrings. They stuck to the front of your earlobe by means of a tiny but powerful magnet on the back of the ear. They looked for all the world like genuine pierced earrings.

My three kids were sitting at the kitchen table having lunch when I casually walked through the kitchen holding a pair of locking pliers on my ear. Amazingly, the children seemed oblivious to this. At first they acted as if it was completely normal for Dad to walk around with a Vise-Grip hanging from his ear.

Several minutes later I sauntered through the kitchen again. But this time I had a grimace on my face, and I was muttering about how this hurt more than I thought it would.

That got their attention. All of it. Their little mouths dropped open. Their eyes grew wide like saucers. Their expressions reflected total bewilderment and then *shock!*

"Daddy's piercing his ears!" shouted my son.

I pulled the vice grip away from my ear and sure enough,

affixed to my left earlobe was a sparkling, diamond-stud pierced earring.

I had a huge grin on my face and asked with as much sincerity as I could muster, "Well, how do I look? Do you like it?"

My boys were stunned and speechless. Lisa, however, got up from the table and immediately demanded to inspect my ear to make sure it wasn't just a fake stick-on. She didn't know about magnetic earrings, and when she saw not only the front but also the metal back, she announced to all in the room that it was real. And then she burst into tears.

That was a reaction that I did not anticipate. I'm not sure what I expected, but I had not intended on upsetting my daughter. I quickly took the earring off and showed her that it was just a joke. She wasn't amused. The guys thought it was great, but my daughter was just plain old mad at Daddy and did she let me know it!

For the next hour, I got the coldest of shoulders from this little girl. No matter what kind of overtures of peace I made, her reaction was the same. Think of cold, hard granite, and that gives you a little idea of what I got from Lisa.

Fortunately, she softened later in the day. She came to me and asked to speak with me in private. I then received a stern lecture from my little girl about how pierced ears were for little girls and not ever for daddies. I was not allowed to leave the room until I gave her my solemn promise to "never ever" pierce my ear.

I truly hadn't planned on any of this. It was mostly a spontaneous instinct that prompted me to put that earring on. You might conclude that I must have a warped sense of inspiration. I won't argue with you, but in the end, Lisa learned something valuable.

She understood that sometimes what you wear on the outside reflects who and what you are on the inside. It wasn't that she disliked pierced ears. The opposite was true. What bothered her was that she was afraid something had fundamentally changed on Daddy's inside. If Daddy decided to wear a pierced earring, it meant that his values had shifted. For children, who desire stability and security, that can be a scary thing.

Lisa was now in a better position to understand my concern for *her* having pierced ears. There is nothing wrong with it. They are fun and look very pretty. But things we buy, places we go, and the things we wear reflect a set of values that can be either right or wrong. We need to be aware of the message our appearance is sending about our inner person.

> Don't be concerned about the outward beauty that depends on jewelry, or beautiful clothes, or hair arrangement. Be beautiful inside, in your hearts, with the lasting charm of a gentle and quiet spirit that is so precious to God. (1 Peter 3:3-4, TLB)

We are not to judge people for the way they look or dress. But we do need to concern ourselves with keeping the inner person clean, holy, and beautiful. If we do this, then the outer person will be just fine.

By the way, I think Lisa looks great with pierced ears.

CHAPTER 5

Mirror, Mirror on the Wall

Most mirrors have the same quality as that famous magical mirror in the story of Snow White. Not all mirrors are magical like that one, but like that mirror, they are obligated to tell the truth. They dutifully reflect back the image of whatever is placed before them.

In our home we had a tall, narrow mirror that stood from floor to well above eye level. It was a truth-telling mirror. This posed no problem at all for my wife because she is, by anyone's standard, a lovely sight to behold. In my case, well, let's just say the truth sometimes hurts, and we'll leave it at that.

I was very interested one day to find one of my children, a toddler at the time, sitting in front of this mirror making faces at himself. I tried to stand out of sight so as not to interrupt but to still be able to observe this child's interaction with his mirror image.

He made a variety of faces at himself, but then to my great

surprise and distress, this child began making a most contorted, angry sort of face and began hissing, *"NO . . . NO . . . NO . . ."* at the reflection in the mirror. I watched in utter amazement as this sweet little child practiced saying the word *no* over and over again. He was getting very good at it too.

I was not a little troubled by this incident and took the matter greatly to heart. It wasn't the "no" part that bothered me. Two-year-olds are notorious for their infatuation with the whole concept of "no." They seem to like the sound and feel of it as they begin exercising their God-given self-will.

What bothered me most about this incident was the faces that went along with it. Under normal circumstances this child had, in the opinion of a definitely prejudiced father, a beautiful face. But what I saw in the mirror was anything but beautiful. It was scary!

My wife and I discussed the whole incident, and we decided not to make too big a deal out of it. We just decided to watch closely and see how it played itself out in the days ahead.

Several days went by, and our household had another incident. I can't even remember what specifically happened, but I distinctly remember that it elicited from me the emotions of anger and hostility. I have a vivid recollection of walking past our truth-telling mirror and, out of the corner of my eye, seeing a reflection. I immediately had the sense that I had seen this reflection somewhere before.

I stopped dead in my tracks, turned squarely to face that mirror, and stared intently at the reflection. After several moments I remembered exactly where I had seen that face. Within moments, that reflection melted away into one of disbelief.

It was just a few days earlier that I had seen that face on

my son, and now, much to my shame, I knew exactly where my son had learned it.

There have been many incidents in my role as a parent that have impressed me, but none has impacted me more than this. I was suddenly struck by the tremendous responsibility that I, as a father, bore in training up this child in the way he should go. I understood that while all my children, because of God's gift of self-will, will ultimately have to stand before him and give an account of their own choices, the way I go about living my life can and will influence the choices they make.

More than a decade has passed since that child sat in front of our mirror, but the lesson to me is as fresh as ever. Even now, if I find I am grieved by my children's patterns of behavior, I can see that they are sometimes a reflection of my own recent behavior, which must be so displeasing to my heavenly Father.

As Christians we claim to reflect Christ. Being Christlike is so very important. The more I can, as a father, reflect Christ in my life, the more likely it is that my children will in turn reflect the Christlike qualities they see in me. This will please both me and my heavenly Father. It is what magnifying the Lord is all about. A life that magnifies God will help people see the true and wonderful qualities that are God's.

> Let your light shine before men in such a way that they may see your good works, and glorify your Father who is in heaven. (Matt. 5:16)

> *My life is but a window,*
> *when others look through me*
> *A glimpse of God's dominion*
> *is what each one will see.*

What will this window show them
about our God above?
Will they see his holiness?
Will they see his love?

Or will he seem a distant blur;
Will he seem far and small?
And might my life be so confused
they don't see him at all?

Oh would that we were spotless
free from sin and clean
so when others look through us
the Savior will be seen.

My life is but a window
and this, O God, I pray
that I would magnify you, Lord
in all I do each day.

PART TWO

Lessons
about
Spiritual
Maturity

CHAPTER 6

When Silence
Is Not Golden

When it comes to children, silence is not always golden. I admit there are those days parents would give anything for a few moments of peace and quiet. Anyone with kids has had his or her share of those days. But notice that the old adage says, "Children should be seen and not heard." It doesn't just say, "Children should not be heard." This is because silent children who are also out of sight often means only one thing: trouble.

Many a time parents have unwittingly been enjoying some peace and quiet when it suddenly dawns on them that they have not seen nor heard from the children for quite some time. Reluctantly, Mom or Dad goes looking for the kids, only to find them at their creative best.

That will be the time the kids have decided to test their hand at cooking pancakes, or maybe they've felt inspired to paint the walls in their bedroom. It could be they've begun excavation of the front yard with a plan to reach

China by lunchtime, and then have the whole afternoon to play with some kids from China. Their motives are often so innocent. How should they know that they shouldn't pick flowers from the neighbor's garden? The flowers were for Mom. Somehow you don't think to tell your kids not to pick the neighbor's flowers until after they've done it.

Every parent should get a list of things to tell their kids before it's too late. Such a list would most certainly contain the following:

- Don't stick raisins up your nose.
- Don't hide your peas in your ears.
- Don't feed the dog peanut butter on potato chips.
- Don't eat soap.
- Don't burn ants with matches.
- Don't go to the bathroom in the neighbor's yard even if their dog goes in ours.
- Don't bring a dead rabbit to school for show-and-tell, even if it is stiff as a board.
- Don't chew gum that's already been chewed.
- Don't jump in the lake with your clothes on.
- Don't close the car door when Daddy's hand is on the door.
- Don't feed your peanut butter sandwich to Daddy's computer.
- Don't flush things down the toilet.
- Don't cut your sister's hair.
- Don't cut your own hair.
- Don't hide under the neighbor's bed.
- Don't beg cookies from the neighbors.
- Don't use crayons on the walls.
- Don't put firecrackers in a bird's nest.

These are just a few of the things I have come up with from experience. If a complete list were to be drawn up from the cumulative experience of all parents, I'm afraid the people who read it might quit having kids altogether. Or if they did have kids, they would keep them locked in their rooms until they grew up and it was safe to let them out.

I can remember one particularly "creative" moment in the lives of my two sons. It was early one Saturday morning. The boys were preschool age, the younger one just a toddler. Usually, the kids were like roosters, up at the crack of dawn, crowing to wake up the rest of the household. However, on this morning, they had climbed out of bed with great stealth to embark on what turned out to be a search-and-destroy mission.

Our awakening that morning turned out to be sudden and alarming. We heard screaming from the downstairs family room. It was the kind of scream that let you know that the crisis was real and imminent. My wife and I both flew down the stairs, not knowing what we'd find when we got there. In my wildest dreams, I could never have imagined what we actually did find.

The family room had, on one wall, a floor-to-ceiling combination cabinet and bookcase. The younger of the two kids was hanging precariously from a shelf two feet from the ceiling. He apparently had developed sufficient skills for climbing but was not at all confident of his ability to get back down. This, then, was the source of the screams. Based on what I saw in the rest of the room, I decided to let him hang there a moment or two longer.

The kids had gotten into the reel-to-reel tape from the tape deck and like the busiest of spiders had woven a web of tangled magnetic tape throughout the entire room. No lamp, no piece of furniture, no drape, not one shelf had been missed. The room had the appearance of one giant spaghetti bowl of magnetic stereo tape.

Early in our marriage, my wife and I had started saving pennies. We stored them in a large glass jar on one of the shelves. The floor was now covered with these pennies. For some reason, the boys had taken to throwing handfuls of them from the jar all around the room. (Weeks later we were still finding pennies in obscure parts of the room and stuck between the furniture cushions.)

There was a great deal more on the shelves to attract kids besides the pennies. My wife kept a prized Hawaiian dried flower arrangement on the shelf. It had been a gift from family and thus had some sentimental value as well. The arrangement featured one particular type of flower that was translucent and shaped like a perfect ball of cotton. My son discovered that these balls would explode when you pinched them, and then they'd release a fine spray of dustlike spores that would float throughout the room. Fascinated with this discovery, he had systematically pinched each and every flower in the arrangement. Only when he had run out of flowers did he realize his predicament of being stuck on the shelf.

His brother, meanwhile, had made his own unique contributions. He had found a set of various colored Magic Markers and decided to work a little magic of his own. He illustrated a few books and redesigned some furniture. Then he turned his attention to his body. Using the colors of bright orange, green, and yellow, this boy painted his little body with Magic Markers. He was not content with this, so he also did a number on his brother. Having yellow, orange, and green bodies is one thing. Green and yellow hair is another. My kids had both.

For my wife and me, seeing all of this at one time had a numbing effect. There was nothing we could say. At some point I rescued the screamer from the top shelf. Other than that, it was not at all clear what we should do next. We were too shocked to be angry. We did think of taking a picture of our two multicolor-striped kids standing there in nothing but their undershorts in the middle of the disaster, but in the end, we decided against it for fear it might positively reinforce the behavior. That was the last thing we wanted to do.

It was only the look on our faces that communicated to the boys the degree of trouble into which they had gotten themselves. They were not entirely sure what the problem was, but they had the good sense to stand there in the middle of the room with their heads down and hands by their sides. If they had had tails, they would have been holding them between their legs.

We spent the rest of the morning doing disaster recovery, and by the end of the day, the room was looking fine. The boys were a different story. Hot baths, soap, and painful scrubbing didn't do much to the Magic Marker stripes, so the next day the boys went to church with green stripes in their hair.

My bottom-line reaction to the events of that morning was one of true wonder at how quickly two innocent little boys could make such a mess. The kids had not meant to do anything wrong. They were just being kids, following their own curiosity and imagination. They didn't set out to get into dangerous situations, destroy things, and create a general disaster of the room. It happened because they lacked the sense and insight that comes with maturity.

Upon further reflection, I had to conclude that the same thing could be said for adults. The only difference is that the size of the mess and the degree of damage can be much more extensive and enduring. As adults, we weave a tangled web of problems in relationships or with destructive patterns of living. We never intend to hurt anyone or create a serious problem. But like children, we just follow our own curiosity and get into something because of its appeal to our spiritually immature nature.

Children are wonderful, but we wouldn't think it natural for them to stay children all of their lives. We want them to grow up into responsible and mature adults. It would be tragic if they never developed physically or mentally. The same thing is true of Christians who don't mature in their faith. Immature Christians can err seriously, make very bad choices, and find themselves in all sorts of precarious situations.

Throughout Scripture, we are admonished to grow in faith and to become spiritually mature.

> When I was a child, I used to speak as a child, think as a child, reason as a child; when I became a man, I did away with childish things. (1 Cor. 13:11)

> As a result, we are no longer to be children, tossed here and there by waves, and carried about by every wind of doctrine, by the trickery of men, by craftiness in deceitful scheming; but speaking the truth in love, we are to grow up in all aspects into Him, who is the head, even Christ. (Eph. 4:14-15)

> Therefore leaving the elementary teaching about the Christ, let us press on to maturity. (Heb. 6:1)

Watching my own children grow and mature has been a very gratifying experience. I can't honestly say that life in our household has gotten any quieter in the process. But we are having fewer "interesting" mornings like the one I have described here. For that I am glad.

CHAPTER 7

The Greatest
of Inventions

God created man. Then God created
woman. And when he did, he decided that women would
get the job of feeding babies in the middle of the night.
That's how it was for thousands of years before some man-
hating inventor came up with bottles and infant formula.
I am convinced that in the natural, created order, it was
never intended that fathers get up in the middle of the
night to feed babies. Baby bottles no doubt are a consequence of the Fall.

I confess that my attitude is utterly despicable. But alas,
my wife will testify that even after three children I have
failed to repent of this character flaw. I should say that my
respect for motherhood has grown immeasurably as I've
observed with wonder my wife getting up time after time,
in the middle of countless nights, to nurse our infants.

One of these occasions will remain steadfast in my memory. It apparently had been a bad night for my wife. The

baby would not go for more than one or two hours without confronting the pains of hunger. He would, accordingly, summon his mother in the manner of all infants. The night-time wail would sound, and she dutifully responded. I, on the other hand, had perfected the art of sleeping with my head under the pillow, thereby insulating my sleep from such disturbances.

On this night, however, it was simply too much for any young mother to deal with. And there I lay, a lump of uncon-sciousness. As my dear wife stood looking down at me, in total frustration she smacked the mattress by my head as hard as she could—and a mother in that state can smack pretty hard. What transpired next was a chiropractor's delight. The way my head snapped back, I was good for monthly adjustments clear into the next century!

Instantly and dramatically roused to consciousness, I found myself confronted by a crying wife in one room and a crying baby in the other. What to do? I asked my wife what had happened. I got the distinct feeling that I had somehow grievously erred and was in need of serious repentance, although I wasn't sure for what. I slunk out of the bedroom and went to aid the crying child. I was equally useless there. This child wanted something I was biologically incapable of rendering.

After waiting what seemed to be a safe amount of time, I hesitantly brought the child to his mother. The time had been sufficient for Mother to get back on an even keel. She gently took the child from my arms, sat down in the rocker, and began to work the magic that mothers have worked on hungry children throughout the ages. I went back to bed, though any chance of sleep had vanished with the past hour's stimulation.

As I lay there, I marveled at how this child had instantly

changed from a wailing intrusion in the night to a beautiful infant resting content in his mother's arms, drawing deeply of the milk that uniquely satisfies. In the quiet of that moment, God's Spirit graciously granted me a wonderful insight.

> Like newborn babes, long for the pure milk of the word, that by it you may grow in respect to salvation. (1 Pet. 2:2)

I was nearly overwhelmed by the power of that teaching. Only now, as I observed firsthand the single-minded, all-consuming desire of a newborn for milk, did I begin to appreciate the truth of this familiar passage, telling how God expects me to long for his Word. No one can rest until the child is satisfied, and there is contentment in nothing other than the mother's milk.

I have been instructed and humbled.

CHAPTER 8

The First Book

I have found that throughout my life, actual experiences don't always match up with my preconceived expectations. Sometimes the experience is better than I expected, and sometimes it falls short. My first crack at reading a book to my son was definitely one of the latter.

I had incredible expectations of what this event was going to be like. There I'd be, sitting on the sofa with this little boy dressed in pajamas plopped on my lap, with a truly great book like *Puppies Are like That*. My oral interpretation was going to be truly spellbinding, especially when I got to the part about the cow. That's where I'd ad-lib with a deep, long, resonant *mmmOOOOOOOOO!* If nothing else, this kid was going to know that his dad could read.

It didn't turn out at all like I had anticipated. I never even got to the part about the cow. Let me explain why.

All of my children have nice, normal names. But early on, each of them had acquired a nickname that tended to fit some personality trait or pattern of behavior they exhibited. This was not at all an intentional sort of thing.

One of my children earned the nickname *Flusher.* This child was fascinated with anything that would swirl and vanish down a toilet. Have you ever tried to flush twelve magazines at once? Flusher did. For entertainment I could take him to a public restroom and let him flush five or six "johns" in a row. By the time he got the last one flushed, the first one was ready to go again. (I lived to regret reinforcing this behavior when it got to the point where he would claim flushing privileges for anyone who used the household privy, family and guests alike.)

When my first child started walking in earnest, he earned the nickname *Tigger.* You all know, of course, what Tiggers do: they bounce. That is precisely what this child did: he bounced. (I have since learned that *all* children are born with disproportionate amounts of energy for the small bodies they have. So they fidget, wiggle, twitch, and—in my son's case—bounce.)

Tigger was a Tigger and simply would not sit still in my lap long enough to read through even a short book. We'd get through a couple of pages with great interest, but then he'd be bouncing off my lap in search of some new attraction. I'd grab the kid and sit him back on my lap for another page or two, and then he'd be off again. On again, off again, on again, off again. No use. We were never going to get to the part about the cow. I finally gave up, and with some disappointment, I set the book down and watched Tigger bounce away, completely oblivious to my feelings.

It wasn't a big deal. But it was at least a little bit of a deal. I wanted to grab the boy, jerk him onto my lap, and tell him, "Hey kid, I'm your father. You're important to me. I've got things to teach you. There are things that you are going to need to know. You should sit still and pay attention. This is a good story. It might even help you learn about how to live."

Then it hit me. It was like being kicked by a mule. *I* was a Tigger, too.

This is just how God must feel about me. He has all these things he wants to tell me. He's got this great book he wants to share with me. And what do I do? I bounce away.

"Dear Father, do you really feel this way about me?"

Cease striving and know that I am God. (Ps. 46:10)

I've heard it explained that God has two ways of demonstrating his power. One way is thunder-and-lightning-type power. The other way is green-grass-and-trees-type power. Creation, the Resurrection, and all of Christ's miracles are examples of his thunder-and-lightning-type power. These manifestations have really been pretty rare throughout the course of history. Most of the time, God has worked in quiet and unspectacular ways.

When God speaks to us, it is much more like his green-grass-and-trees-type power. You can't see the trees grow, but years of steady, silent development bring about the solid, mature trees.

He speaks to us through his Word and the Holy Spirit. It is this constant and quiet nurturing that we need to listen to. He seldom shouts at us. We need to be still and quiet to listen.

It's surprising what you can learn from a book about puppies.

CHAPTER 9

Fort Dearborn

In fourth grade, throughout much of the
United States, children embark upon that infamous fourth-
grade project, The State Report. I have consulted with
enough teachers and parents to understand that this represents a monumental challenge to students and parents
alike. It is a comprehensive endeavor, complete with art-
work, historical summaries, maps, biographies, class plays,
and, yes, the diorama. The diorama is a scene constructed
in a shoe box or its equivalent, which is intended to depict
some significant feature or event in the history of the state
being studied. For our school, the diorama seemed to be
the crowning achievement of the entire project.

My son had decided that he wanted to construct a model
of Fort Dearborn. He had, I guess, been quite taken by the
history of Indian wars in Illinois and the role Fort Dearborn
had played in some of those wars.

My own days spent in Christian Service Brigade served me

well, because I was quite familiar with blockhouses, stockades, and forts in general. We also had some good artists' depictions of what the original fort looked like. I suggested to my son that he could use wooden matches as the basic building material. He agreed, so I began the task of removing the match heads from hundreds of wooden matches.

Things went quite well until I got the bright idea of speeding up the decapitation process by using my table jigsaw. I tried to cut the heads off a bundle of ten to fifteen matches at a crack. I'd hold them in one hand and run the whole bundle through the saw. Well, it wasn't the first dumb thing I've done in my life, and it certainly hasn't been the last. As you might have already guessed, I misjudged the distance a bit and wound up igniting fifteen match heads at once while clutching them tightly in my fingers. Yes, I burned my fingers. Yes, it hurt. Yes, I'm all right now. There wasn't the slightest bit of permanent damage.

Now this was supposed to be an educational project. I've concluded that dioramas were invented to bring out the "dumb" in fathers. This gives the children hope that if Dad survived in this world long enough to grow up, then surely the kid is going to make it too.

The remainder of the evening was, in my mind, simply terrific. This turned out to be an entire-family project. All of the kids got involved in gluing the little sticks together to make the walls of the stockade. My fourth-grade son directed the project and did the tricky part of constructing the blockhouses and interior buildings. Several hours later, I had to say that the fort was really taking shape. In fact, it looked just great.

I watched with tremendous satisfaction as my son added the last of the match sticks. This was terrific. All of us had gotten involved. The project was done and looked remarkably like the picture. It even had a little flag sticking up like the one in the book! I was smiling from my heart to my ears, but as I turned to look at my son, I sensed that he did not share my pleasure in this moment.

"What's wrong, Son? Don't you like it?"

"Well, Dad . . ."

"Well, what? I think it looks great, Son."

"But, Dad, it's not quite right."

"What do you mean? It looks just like the picture!"

"Dad, can we burn it?"

"What?!"

I couldn't believe what I had just heard. Here we had spent all this time building a great fort, and now he wants to burn it. It didn't make any sense at all.

"Son, why in the world would you want to burn this up?"

My son went on to explain that in this particular battle, the Indians had won and had burned down Fort Dearborn. So we had to burn it.

This illustrates the difference in the thinking between a fourth-grade boy and a dad. It made absolutely no sense to me to waste an entire evening's effort, especially when the effort had been so productive.

I was about to do something foolish and veto this proposal, but instead—to my surprise—I did something that smacked of good sense. I kept my mouth shut and tried to understand my son's point of view. I thought about it, and . . . it still didn't make any sense to me. In the end, I concluded that, after all, it wasn't my project. It didn't have to make any sense to me. It only had to make sense to my son.

We took it outside and torched it.

I stood there watching the evening's work literally go up in smoke. It was about half gone when my son shouted to me, "OK, Dad, that's enough!"

"That's enough what?"

"That's enough burning!"

The next few moments were a bit of a panic as we went about the process of saving the fort. In the end we were successful in saving about half of it. There it stood, a charred, soaked mess of whatever. I glanced at my son. He was beaming.

"It's perfect, Dad, really awesome!"

My son came home from school the next day with glowing reports about how all the kids thought his diorama was cool and awesome and all the other superlatives common to that age. I was amazed.

Several weeks later, at a PTA function, I happened to meet my son's teacher in the school hallway. We stopped and exchanged greetings, she said a few kind things about having my son in her class, and I thanked her for her good work on our behalf. We had started to head our separate ways when she stopped and, as an afterthought, said, "By the way, your son's diorama was really wonderful. The children all loved it. What a creative idea to burn it like that!"

Once again it became apparent to me that I am not always right. In this case, my fourth-grade son knew better than his dad. I was amazed at how blind I had been to the positive effect burning the fort would have. I suppose it was because I had invested so much of myself in its construction that I couldn't see how burning up my work could possibly help.

I learned at least two lessons in all of this. One is that sometimes my heavenly Father wants to burn up something in my life to make it just right. I react just like I did with my son. "You've got to be kidding, Lord!" But God knows what the final picture is really supposed to look like, and sometimes it requires burning up things I care about—things I've built just the way I think they should be. If I can learn to behave in these instances, like I did with the fort, I am going to be better for it. I don't have to insist on understanding it all right away. I need to trust the circumstances to God, who knows everything and truly wants the best for me.

One of the things that bothered me about this affair was that I was perfectly willing to help as long as it was going like I expected and wanted it to go. When things started moving in a different direction, I really started begrudging my help in the project. I wanted to interact with my son in a way that suited *me*, even though it was really his project.

Sometimes we relate to God this way. A relationship with God is fine as long as it goes like we want it to. I knew of a person who struggled in his relationship with God because of the doctrine of hell. To this individual, hell was inconsistent with what he wanted God to be. His god was a loving god and, therefore, could never send anybody to hell. He had drawn a box around what God should be, and the God of the Bible didn't fit the box. Rejection of the Bible and God as presented in his Word was the natural consequence. Just as I needed to submit to my son's ideas for his fort, we need to submit to God's plans for our lives and to his revelation of who he is and what he wants—even when that means "burning up" things we think are just fine the way they are.

Like my son did, God can see the end result better than we can.

> We know that God causes all things to work together for good to those who love God, to those who are called according to His purpose. (Rom. 8:28)

CHAPTER 10

Masters of Timing

It had been a good day at work for me. I was glad to come home and was looking forward to a nice evening with my family. That's the first thing a kid looks for when he has to deliver bad news. *Dad's in a good mood.*

And after dinner, one of my sons took advantage of the mood.

"Dad, can I talk to you?"

I looked up from the latest issue of *Reader's Digest* to see a small boy stooped over with the weight of some invisible burden. I waited for him to speak. No words came. He just stood there, silently staring at his toes.

"Well, Son, didn't you say that you have something we need to talk about?"

"Yes."

This affirmative response was followed by more awkward moments of silence with his eyes still riveted toward the floor.

"It's OK, Son, go ahead and tell me what's on your mind."

I tried to sound encouraging, although from the looks of the situation at that point, a sense of impending doom began to press in around me.

With a few faltering verbal steps, my son began the woeful tale.

"Dad, ya know Steven?"

"Yes, I know Steven, my son, your brother. What about Steven?"

"Well, he made me do it!"

"What did he make you do?"

"Our car, ya know our car?"

I braced myself for what was to come next.

"Yes, I know our car. What about our car?"

"Steven made me pick the lock."

"What lock?"

"The lock on the door of the car."

"And what happened when you picked the lock?"

My son proceeded to meekly relate to me the whole story of how he and his brother were playing and were inspired with the bright idea that they could pick the lock of the car with just a paper clip. The only problem was that the paper clip had broken deep inside the lock mechanism and was forever irretrievable. I could no longer insert a key into the lock. Ultimately this meant that one had to get into the passenger's side of the car and slide over to the driver's side. The alternative was to have the car repaired, which required replacement of the entire locking system in the car doors, new keys, and big bucks.

I sat there and listened to this tale as it came trickling out. I thought first about the cost of repair. Then I thought about the cost of a simple paper clip. It just didn't seem fair. Frustration began to build. I went on to ask one of those amazingly dumb questions that parents have asked since

the beginning of time and will go on asking for generations
to come.

"Why did you do that?"

If you're smiling right now, it's because you've been there.
You too have asked this dumb question. It's dumb because
there is no real answer, and it wouldn't do a bit of good
even if there was. It's just that in the face of the absurd and
irrational, we have a deep longing to somehow make sense
out of a senseless situation. We need to know why these
things happen.

"I already told you, Dad. I did it because Steven made me
do it."

"How did he make you do it? Did he threaten you with a
nuclear bomb?"

"No."

"Did he say he was going to pulverize you with a baseball
bat?"

"No."

"Did he force you with a machine gun?"

"No."

"Well then, help me understand. How did he make you
do it?"

"I dunno. He just told me to do it and I did. When I stuck
the paper clip in the keyhole and turned it, it broke."

This was an unsatisfying explanation in my opinion, but
what could you expect from a six-year-old would-be lock
picker?

I saw two problems at this point. The first was that I
now was the owner of a car with only one of its two doors
working properly. This was a somewhat inconvenient
and expensive, but otherwise unimportant, problem.
The second was considerably more important. I was not
pleased with my son's failure to own up to his share of the

responsibility in the failed attempt to pick the lock. He was himself unadmittedly intrigued with the task and would probably have made the attempt to do so even without his older brother's encouragement.

I believe we all need to take responsibility for our mistakes, and up to this point, my son had not done that. This was not an issue of moral wrong, but a simple case of misjudgment typical of young children. My son made a mistake, partially admitted it, and attempted to duck his share of the responsibility. What this left me with was one of those "teachable moments" that parenting books tell you to take advantage of.

I went to inspect the damage, which confirmed the worst-case scenario. This only served to add to my enthusiasm for the teaching to come. When I found my son, however, my resolve quickly wilted when his eyes met mine.

They say that the eyes are the window to the soul, and when I looked down into his big brown ones, I saw a little boy's soul full of apprehension, turmoil, regret, and true remorse for his mistake. His apology and request for forgiveness came sputtering through his attempt to choke back his tears.

There was nothing to say to this child. All that remained to do was to pick him up and give him one of those good daddy bear hugs, the kind that doesn't say anything but at the same time says everything: *All is forgiven. It's OK. You're OK. You are loved. It's safe to be near me. Yes, you can still live here.*

Further reflection on this throughout the remainder of the evening helped me understand something of how my heavenly Father feels when I come to him, confessing my mistakes. All too often I have someone else to blame, like Adam in Genesis 3, who said, "It's that woman you gave me."

Or like Eve: "It's that serpent's fault." Sometimes I react like the proud and unrighteous Pharisee who stood before God in the temple and said:

> God, I thank Thee that I am not like other people: swindlers, unjust, adulterers, or even like this tax-gatherer. (Luke 18:11)

I can always find someone else who is a little or even a lot "worse" than I am, and in so doing, I deceive myself into a false sense of justification.

What God wants is a broken and contrite heart (Ps. 51:17). He doesn't say "broken people." He says broken and contrite *hearts*. Hearts broken from sin become the foundation for lives of tremendous strength. The strongest people in this world are those with the softest hearts when it comes to recognizing their own sin. The apostle Paul was a man of incredible strength of character and spirit. He also thought of himself as the foremost of sinners.

I know how I felt when my son tried to duck his responsibility. I also know how I felt when I saw and understood his genuine remorse for his mistake. It did turn out to be one of those golden teachable moments that you read about in parenting books. It was, however, my heavenly Father who did the teaching, and in the end, it was I who was instructed.

CHAPTER 11

Never Ever . . .

Turn down that music!"
"Keep your hands to yourself."
"Chew with your mouth closed."
"Don't use your outside voice inside the house."

These are all examples of universal commands that every parent in the world will invoke at one time or another. I also believe it's fair to say that each of these commands will be used much more than once in the process of bringing a child to adulthood.

Kids have a great ability to interpret the various directives they receive from parents and to sort out which ones need to be strictly adhered to and which ones give them some room for maneuvering. For instance, imagine a family driving down the highway at sixty-five miles an hour with the kids in the backseat poking and provoking one another in a way that leads to either an outburst of tears or a tumult of high-pitched giggles. Dad, in the front seat, issues Universal Command #17:

"You kids sit still!"

The father might even combine it with Universal Command #23:

"You kids sit still and be quiet!"

At first blush these directives appear perfectly clear, but if you stop to analyze them with a kid's brain, you'll see that there is really a great deal of ambiguity involved. Literal compliance to the father's command is a bit hard to imagine. Does it mean kids shouldn't blink their eyes or even breathe? Should they stop their hearts from beating? Should they totally refrain from any further audible expression to communicate legitimate needs for the bathroom? No. What the dad is really saying is that there is too much noise and commotion in the car for his liking, and it is his strong preference that there be less of this kind of annoyance.

Kids know this is not really a command, but a request to modify morally neutral behavior in order to conform to a parent's wishes. Kids can't say it in these words, but they understand just the same. What usually happens is that there is a temporary behavior modification, then the old patterns begin to escalate once more until the "commands" are reissued along with some threat of sanction. (These sanctions, by the way, are seldom enforceable while going sixty-five miles an hour down the highway, and the kids know that too.)

Again, any compliance to the parent's wishes is short-lived, and back and forth it goes until the parent reaches the breaking point. When that happens, language is used that communicates clearly to a child that a *real* command has been issued. Total compliance is now necessary to avoid the certain impending penalty for failure to obey.

In our household we use the words *never ever* to communicate to the kids that whatever proceeds next from Mom or

Dad's mouth needs to be strictly adhered to. We are careful not to overuse *never ever* so our kids can distinguish between expressions of preference and commands that warrant immediate and total compliance.

With that as background, you can better understand my reaction one day when I heard my wife exclaim: "Never ever!"

I was downstairs in the basement at the time, working on some project, when I heard the words. I immediately paused to hear what was coming next.

"Never ever!"

That was two *never evers*. Whatever was coming next must really be something.

"Never ever!"

That was *three,* a new record! And with that I was bounding up the stairs to see what in the world was going on. I had just reached the top of the stairs when I heard the rest of the command:

"NEVER EVER use a pizza cutter on top of your baby brother's head!"

It was true. Our two-year-old son had gotten hold of a pizza cutter, and my wife found him sitting on top of his nine-month-old brother, rolling the pizza cutter up and down the baby's head. Now that's a definite four-*never-ever* if there ever was one. The baby suffered no lasting damage, but he does have a permanent part in his hair right down the middle of his head.

Unfortunately, children are not the only ones with the ability to ignore directives and commands. Adults can be quite accomplished at this as well. We can be especially adept at ignoring our heavenly Father's commands.

Every man and woman is born with a conscience. Our conscience is one of the ways that God speaks to us to let us know his wishes and desires in a situation. But we have the power to choose to obey or not. If we repeatedly ignore God in this way, there comes a point when our ability to hear—our conscience—becomes seriously impaired. Scripture refers to this process when Paul, writing to Timothy, says:

> The Spirit explicitly says that in later times some will fall away from the faith, paying attention to deceitful spirits and doctrines of demons, by means of the hypocrisy of liars seared in their own conscience as with a branding iron. (1 Tim. 4:1-2)

When skin is seared with a branding iron, it leaves scarred tissue that has no feeling. The nerve endings have been destroyed.

My wife and I honeymooned on Mackinac Island, a small resort island in the northern waters of the Great Lakes. We didn't know it when we made the reservations, but this island was the destination for the Chicago to Mackinac sailboat race held every July. Our honeymoon coincided with the race, and we were probably the only nonboaters on the island that week.

We had spent our first day on the island touring some of the historic sites. The island had held some strategic military importance in the history of the United States, and we had seen its fort and heard about some of the island's historical significance in the wars among Indians, France, Britain, and the United States.

That night, my wife and I were literally blasted from our sleep when a cannon went off outside our window. I had no idea what was going on, but my first thought was that the island was being attacked by the French. I was about ready to dismiss it all as an unusually vivid dream when we were shaken by a second blast. I had expected fireworks on my honeymoon, but nothing like this!

I looked out the window, and in the moonlight I could just distinguish the billowing sails of two boats on the lake. Why were they shooting at these boats? I later discovered that these were the first of hundreds of boats that would cross the finish line of the Chicago to Mackinac race. Every time a boat crossed the finish line, a cannon would fire in salute of its accomplishment. Sailboats continued to cross the line for the next three days. That's seventy-two straight hours of periodic cannon blasts outside our window.

I didn't sleep well the rest of that night. Each blast would jar me like a bolt of lightning. But the amazing thing was that by the third day, neither my wife nor I were bothered in the least by the cannons blasting away. After two days of firing we were able to effectively ignore it.

The same thing can happen to people with the cannons of God. Those first salvos jar us and jolt us and grab our attention in a way that can even prevent us from sleeping. But when we continually choose to ignore them, following our own desires instead of God's, there will come a day when we will lose our ability to hear. Our consciences will, in fact, be seared.

Parents will sometimes ask in jest if a child has lost his hearing because that is just how it appears when a directive has been ignored. The kids act as if they didn't hear a word that was said. If we truly suspected that there was something wrong with our child's hearing, we wouldn't hesitate to take that child to a doctor for an examination of the ears. I think we would all do well to structure into our lives periodic examinations of our spiritual hearing. We need to recognize that our hearing isn't what it used to be, and then, with repentance, ask God to restore it to a full measure. Spiritual hearing loss is never permanent with God.

CHAPTER 12

A Not-So-Great Bike Ride

There are several things about parenting that no one tells you about until after you have kids yourself. Only after you are well into the experience of raising children do they let you know about it, and then, of course, it's too late. Teaching kids to ride a two-wheeled bicycle is one example of what I'm talking about. They give you these things called "training wheels," along with a handshake and wish for good luck, and then leave it up to your own imagination to figure out just how to get the job done.

I tried to remember how I was taught to make the transition from a bike equipped with training wheels to one without, but frankly it was so long ago that I had completely forgotten. Judging by my own children's experience, it is more likely that I simply blocked the whole episode from my memory and could only recover it with $17,000 of counseling sessions that explored the deepest repressions of my childhood.

When teaching my second son how to ride, I opted for the downhill, let-gravity-do-the-work method. I hadn't discovered this method with my first son. In his case, I just held on to the back of the bicycle seat, steadying the bike, while I ran alongside him. Because the bike was so low, I had to run all hunched over. It took a long time for the boy to learn how to ride that summer. This was good and bad. The good part was that I ran myself into shape. The bad part was that the shape I ran myself into approximated a pretzel. It was for this reason that I decided to go with gravity the second time around.

I took my second son to the top of a long, steady slope. Rather than run behind him, I thought I'd just let gravity supply the force to keep the bike's momentum going forward instead of falling to the side. *Bad idea.* The forward part worked just fine—gravity did its job and kept the bike moving downhill. The problem occurred when it came to stopping at the bottom. As it turned out, a fire hydrant intervened and brought my son to a sudden and painful stop.

I saw it coming and was running hard after the boy, but I failed to reach him before the impact of flesh and bone against cold, hard iron. It wasn't pretty. I scooped up my son from the ground and expected the worst. It was bad, but the kid was stoic. He wanted to cry but wouldn't do it. Rubbing his bruised arms and legs, he picked up the bike and headed for the top of the hill. The next time down, I ran alongside him, and we managed to avoid every hazard along the way. It was in this manner that my second son learned how to ride his bike.

Flush with confidence, I decided to take the entire family out for a family bike ride. This was the first time that both of our boys would be riding their own bikes. My daughter, still too young to ride on her own, was perched on the back of

my bike in a seat designed exactly for that purpose. I took
the lead, my wife took up the rear, and the boys filled in
between us. Like ducks in a row, we headed out on our little
expedition. Our destination was Grandma and Grandpa's
house—a little more than a mile from our home. It was a bit
ambitious for a first outing, but with a little extra effort, I
was sure we could manage it.

Things were going remarkably well, and we were within a
block of our destination when I heard that distinctive sound
of metal on metal. I braked to a stop and looked behind me
to see what had happened. Our number three "duck" had
somehow managed to smack into the rear end of a car. He
had missed the bumper and hit where you can do some real
damage to a car. And the car was new. Brand-new. It still had
the licensed-applied-for sticker on it.

"What happened to the boy?" you ask. The fact that I men-
tioned first the damage to the car reveals all too clearly my
flaws as a father. My first and immediate concern, I'm
ashamed to admit, was for the liability that I now faced for
my son's damage to this brand-new automobile. It wasn't
that I was unconcerned about my son's welfare, but with an
immediate and quick appraisal of the situation, I concluded
that he was going to be OK. It was the damage to the car
that occupied my attention at that moment.

What had started out with such great expectations and
had, up until this point, gone so well was now starting to
unravel. I felt frustrated. What does a normal man do in
a situation like this? You blame your wife, that's what you do.

"Honey!" I said, "I thought you were supposed to be watching out for the kids! How come you let Mark run into the
car like that?"

Sometimes I really amaze myself with how dumb I can
be. Blaming my wife for this must be the ultimate example

of DUMB. It was totally unrealistic to expect Ruthie to have somehow anticipated that Mark would fail to see a parked car in his path. He had successfully negotiated many obstacles in our trip up to this point. He was just following the simple instructions that *I* had given him: to ride as close to the side of the road as possible. We were riding past a park, and Mark was evidently watching the kids play in the park rather than concentrating on where he was going.

The truth of the matter was that I had not done a good job of leading. I should have thought to warn my son that he needed to adjust his course. I should have warned him to follow me. I should have been more diligent in checking to see that he was paying attention to where he was going instead of being distracted.

I learned several lessons as a result of this event. I learned how much it costs to repair a new car that has been rear-ended by a bicycle. I learned that these accidents are not covered by any of my insurance policies. But more important, I learned an immense lesson from the owner of that car.

He had been playing with his kids in the park but came walking over to the car when he saw the pileup. Unlike mine, *his* first question concerned the welfare of my son. He valued people more than things, and his immediate concern for Mark reflected his priorities. He couldn't have been happy about the damage to his car, but it was, after all, just metal, plastic, rubber, and other synthetic materials. He was kind and forgiving, and he graciously accepted our apologies and restitution. He was a class act all the way.

I also learned to appreciate the dilemma our heavenly Father faces when he tries to lead his children through life. Sometimes his children become distracted and don't keep their eyes on the Father's leading. It is then that we are most likely to crash in life. Life has its potential dangers, and the

Father wants to lead us around them and get us safely to our destination. Failure on our part to obey his instructions and follow his lead jeopardizes the successful completion of our journey.

Fortunately for us, the Father's leading is perfect, and his priority of concerns is never suspect. Because of this, we can live life with confidence. What a great ride!

> How can a young man keep his way pure? By keeping it according to Thy word. With all my heart I have sought Thee; do not let me wander from Thy commandments. . . . I am a stranger in the earth; do not hide Thy commandments from me. (Ps. 119:9-10, 19)

> Your ears will hear a word behind you, "This is the way, walk in it," whenever you turn to the right or to the left. (Isa. 30:21)

CHAPTER 13

We're Gonna Tip

My wife tells me that I am the adventure-some sort. This is a polite way of saying that I am dumb enough to try most things at least once. I offer the following anecdote in support of my wife's claims.

Our young family was on vacation at a summer camp run by the school where I teach. The weather that summer was wonderful, and our family vacation was progressing in splendid fashion. We had a lakeside cabin, and for many days we had enjoyed watching all of the waterfront activities. I was especially taken by the sailboats as I watched the brightly colored sails billow, full of lake breeze, impelling the small boats across the water. It looked so peaceful and inviting.

Needless to say, I was delighted when a colleague of mine from the physics department invited me to join him sailing one afternoon. I didn't know the first thing about rigging a sailboat or what to do with it once you got going, but I figured my physicist friend would teach me all I needed to know. Unfortunately, he didn't know anything about sailing either.

This is where adventuresome (or dumb, depending on your perspective) comes in. We decided that we ought to be able to figure this thing out, so we looked at a few diagrams at the boat dock, observed a few boats out on the lake, and then went for it.

As it turned out, we got the rigging nearly correct, and with the advice of some kind students we met out on the lake, we even managed to perfect it. As for what to do when we got on the lake, we relied on my colleague's intrinsic knowledge of the laws of physics to guide us.

For a considerable while, we got along just fine. But my friend must have forgotten some very basic law of physics because suddenly, without much warning, we found ourselves very wet and with an inverted sailboat to boot. I have already admitted that I knew very little about sailing, but even I knew that to be successful at this sort of thing, one should really have the sail pointing up out of the water rather than straight down below the boat.

I began wishing I had paid more attention in all my physics courses because, try as he might, my physicist friend couldn't muster up enough knowledge of the laws of nature to get us righted. Finally, some kid in a speedboat came roaring up, quickly appraised the situation, jumped into the water, and had the sailboat righted within a matter of moments. (He obviously had had a good and recent course in physics, and thankfully, he must have paid attention to his studies.) With gratitude in our hearts and water in our sneakers, we sailed back to the boat dock without further incident. We arrived wetter, somewhat wiser, and definitely more humble.

Not to be discouraged by one little mishap, we tried it

again a few days later and pulled it off without tipping our boat. We arrived back as dry as when we left. This experience boosted my confidence to the point where I decided it was time to share this great experience of sailing with my two young boys.

The moment I broke the news to Steven and Mark they looked at each other and said in unison, "He's gonna tip us." They said it so stoically and so matter-of-factly that it caught me completely off guard. They had absolutely no confidence in my abilities as a sailor, but they resigned themselves to the fact that it was their duty as children to go "have fun" with Dad, even if it meant they were going to be miserable.

With every ten steps or so toward the boat dock, they managed to work into the conversation their prediction that we were "gonna tip." No matter how cheerful and confident I tried to be, they were convinced that we were doomed to get wet. I was somewhat irritated by the amount of time and care the boys spent in selecting their life jackets, but I let the matter pass without comment.

After selecting the proper craft and rigging it carefully, we launched out to have some real fun.

Guess what the boys' last words were as we shoved off. . . .

I was bound and determined to make this thing a smashing success, and we almost made it too. We were on our way in when that one last gust of fickle wind hit us. As we were headed over, the boys calmly and resolutely sounded what had by now become an all too familiar refrain: "We're gonna tip!"

We did. And we remained in that state until some kindly grandparent-type folks in a pontoon boat came by to help extricate us from our predicament. The boys climbed on board their boat and tried to stay warm while they towed us a short distance back to camp.

We walked back to the cabin and were met by my wife. My boys greeted her with three simple words: "Dad tipped us."

There was not the least bit of malice in their voices. It was just a statement of fact, which they accepted with grace and dignity.

The fact that my boys went with me that day, believing what they did, will forever be one of the most meaningful things they could have done for me. Even though they believed—as it turned out, rightly so—that we were going to tip over and get cold and wet, they had been willing to give it a go because they sensed it was something I wanted us to do together. They knew better than I what the result was going to be and that it wouldn't be all that fun, but their lack of confidence in my sailing abilities was overshadowed by their commitment to me.

> Only be very careful to observe the commandment and the law which Moses the servant of the Lord commanded you, to love the Lord your God and walk in all His ways and keep His commandments and hold fast to Him and serve Him with all your heart and with all your soul. (Josh. 22:5)

> Though the fig tree should not blossom, and there be no fruit on the vines, though the yield of the olive should fail, and the fields produce no food, though the flock should be cut off from the fold, and there be no cattle in the stalls, yet I will exult in the Lord, I will rejoice in the God of my salvation. The Lord God is my strength, and He has made my feet like hinds' feet, and makes me walk on my high places. (Hab. 3:17-19)

There is no substitute for commitment. I understand in a new way what my commitment to the heavenly Father can mean to him. Some things in life I will do because I want to. They will be pleasing to me and much to my liking. I also understand that some things in life I will do because they serve the pleasure of my heavenly Father. They may not be so fun for me. They may not be to my liking. But I will do them because I am committed to the Father. In doing so, I know just how pleased he will be.

I've done a fair amount of sailing since that time.

No, I don't make the boys come with me.

CHAPTER 14

Maul Ball

There's an old joke about the wife who was upset when her husband came home several hours late from his Saturday golf outing.

"Where on earth have you been? You can't possibly have been playing golf all this time!"

The husband responded, "I'm sorry, honey, but George had a heart attack and dropped dead on the third hole."

Of course the wife was upset by this tragic news and immediately felt some remorse for having snapped so quickly at her husband. With a most sincere voice she responded, "Oh, I'm so sorry, dear. That must have been just terrible."

To which her husband responded, "It sure was! It was hit the ball, drag George, hit the ball, drag George, hit the ball, and drag George again for the next fifteen holes!"

The story illustrates the extent to which people can become involved in athletic pursuit. Dragging around a person is a common occurrence in our family when we play "maul ball."

Maul ball is really a senseless game, but my kids like it. We play it often in the winter when there is a good deal of snow on the ground. One person picks up a football and begins running around the yard until he is tackled. After he's tackled, the ball is thrown up for grabs and recovered by another player, who then runs around until he is mauled. (I told you it was senseless.)

The children especially seem to enjoy mauling dear old Dad. I don't run; I just walk very deliberately around the yard and let the kids try to bring me down. At first, they would try to get as many kids as they could hanging on to my neck. While this was somewhat effective in limiting my oxygen intake, I could remain on my feet for long periods of time by just making sure I kept my feet spread apart, forming a solid base of support.

They have since found that a better strategy for bringing down an adult is to designate one of the attackers to be the "claw." It is the task of the claw to come in low and lock on to one of Dad's legs and not let go. This weakens the base considerably and makes Dad very vulnerable to attacks on the upper body, which sends him crashing to the earth, much to the children's delight and satisfaction.

If I am to have any success at all, I must guard against the assault of the claw. Once hooked, there is no escape. I am convinced that I could drag a kid clamped on to my leg for hours without getting him to let go. The tenacity with which kids will stick to my leg never ceases to amaze me. Wherever I go, they go. I'll take a step and drag the claw, take a step, drag the claw, take another step and drag the claw, until the other maulers topple me over.

The claw strategy, while not recommended for golf, is a

very good strategy for maul ball. It is also a good strategy for living a successful life. This became clear to me when, after a recent game of maul ball, I read a Bible passage about King Hezekiah.

> He trusted in the Lord, the God of Israel; so that after him there was none like him among all the kings of Judah, nor among those who were before him. For he clung to the Lord; he did not depart from following Him, but kept His commandments, which the Lord had commanded Moses. And the Lord was with him; wherever he went he prospered. (2 Kings 18:5-7)

Hezekiah's steadfast grasp on the Lord ensured his success in all of his endeavors. By always holding on to God, he would always find himself following the will of God. He would automatically go wherever God would lead.

The image of one of my children locked on to my leg, holding on tenaciously no matter where I go, is a wonderful picture for me as I think about how God wants me to live my life. In the same way, I must cling to the Father and never let go.

That seems to me to be the best strategy there is for going through life without getting mauled.

THREE

Lessons
about God

CHAPTER 15

Visit of the Slammer

It was somewhere between midnight and four in the morning. There was, as far as I could tell, no sound. And yet—there was some sort of disturbance in the deep rhythm of my sleep. I could sense it. Slowly I raised my eyelids to half-mast, and there he was. It was a small child of three standing at my bedside, just staring at me.

"Is that you, Son?"

"Yes, Daddy."

"What do you want?"

"Nothing, Daddy."

"Go back to bed."

"OK, Daddy."

And with that, the little man turned and headed back to his room. My eyelids dropped shut, and I attempted to avoid processing the last few moments in my mind.

It didn't work.

Just who was this little person, anyway? Was it really one of my children, or could it have been some character from a dream? Did this really happen at all? *Don't think about it. Just get back to sleep.* But my brain kept processing on autopilot, and it became clearer to me that all of this did really happen and that this little person was indeed my first son, the son I had nicknamed *Slammer.* This boy had developed a liking for slamming doors, drawers, cabinets, and anything that would open and close. He would systematically open all the drawers in the kitchen or all the cabinets in the family room and then, one by one, slam them shut like a string of firecrackers. This was not behavior that, as parents, we appreciated or encouraged. In fact, we attempted to discourage it and at times enforced painful sanctions for its display. But the behavior still persisted for some time.

As I lay there in bed, the thought that this was indeed a visit by Slammer solidified in my mind like a slab of quicksetting concrete. I then quickly calculated that there were two doors between my bed and Slammer's bed. Instinct took over. I ripped off the bed covers, leaped out of bed, and took an angle to the bedroom door in hopes of heading off the slammer.

BOOM!

Too late for the first door.

BOOM!

He got them both.

The reason for my concern regarding doors slamming in the middle of the night was lying asleep in a crib next to the Slammer's room: a baby named Mark. Mark had two ways of waking up in the middle of the night. Sometimes he would wake up crying. This generally was not a problem because he was seldom fully awake in this unhappy state. It was relatively easy to go into his room, pat him on the "popo" or rock him a short while, and back to sleep he'd go. The other way he'd wake up was insidious. He would, with the sweetest singsong of voices, call "Daaaa-dy, Daaa-dy." At seven o'clock in the morning, there could be no sweeter sound on earth. But in the middle of the night it was a siren warning of impending disaster. Because if I was being beckoned by the sweet melody of "Daaa-dy," it meant that I was being summoned for one thing only. That was to *play*. Now I love to play with my kids as much as anyone, but not in the middle of the night.

There I was, frozen in suspense at what would happen next. What would come from Mark's room? I held my breath and waited.

"Daaa-dy, Daaa-dy, . . . Daaaa-aaaaa-aaaaa-dy."

That was it. Hope of any sleep for the next several hours melted away into the darkness of the night. I, the zombie daddy, trudged into Mark's room. In the glow of the nightlight I could see his gummy little smile stretched ear to ear and his eyes reflecting the sparkle of the starlight. He was standing in the corner of the crib, bouncing on the mattress. He was definitely ready to play.

I grabbed Mark and thought I'd better check on the perpetrator of this situation. I went into Slammer's room. There he was, sound asleep in his bed as if none of this had ever happened. My feelings at that moment were a tossed salad of envy, frustration, self-pity, satisfaction, and wonder. I envied his sleep. I was frustrated that I'd been wakened for no apparent reason. It seemed unfair that Slammer could go back to sleep and I could not. I have always derived a real sense of satisfaction from the sight of my children sleeping contentedly. He certainly was content; I was not. I was awake in the middle of the night with a kid who wanted to play.

I had time that night, while playing with Mark, to reflect on what brought Slammer to my bedside in the first place.

He didn't seem to want anything other than knowing that I was there. How long had he been standing there? My thoughts drifted to recollections of my own childhood and the comfort that came to me with the knowledge that I could sleep in peace because my father was there. As I thought about these things, I felt my limitations as a father. Slammer came to me and found me sleeping. And yet he seemed to draw comfort even from a sleeping father.

These thoughts led me to a new appreciation for my heavenly Father. When I go to him in the middle of the night, I will never find him sleeping.

> He who keeps you will not slumber. Behold, He who keeps Israel will neither slumber nor sleep. (Ps. 121:3-4)

This is a good lesson for all kids—little and grown-up ones alike—to know. So now when my kids go to sleep, I try to help them understand that God, our heavenly Father, is still awake and watching over us. Bedtime prayers have been a natural part of human tradition since anyone can remember. I believe they have been motivated in large part by people's innate longing to rest in the security of a watchful and loving God. We can go to sleep knowing full well that God will not. What good news this is for troubled people living in these days.

> In peace I will both lie down and sleep, for Thou alone, O Lord, dost make me to dwell in safety. (Ps. 4:8)

CHAPTER 16

Life's Merry-go-rounds

It was truly a "kiddie kingdom." This place was great. Most of the rides were just a quarter, and already a quarter wasn't all that much money. The rides were all pretty tame. I'm the kind that can turn four shades of green just *thinking* about theme park attractions, but I could go on most of these things and even almost like them. Our preschool-age kids absolutely loved the place.

The evening was perfect. Cool summer breezes came drifting in and washed away the heat of the late afternoon. Flying conditions were ideal for the helicopter ride. This was the ride with a circle of helicopters, each equipped with its own control stick that let you make it go up and down as you chased the enemy before you and evaded the one behind. On the front of each of the helicopters was a machine gun that swiveled in the hands of trigger-happy flyers.

There were four adults and five kids in our group. This wasn't what you would consider an unwieldy number of folks to keep track of, so we weren't all that hyper about keeping tabs on everyone. But as so often happens, when the ride was over and we counted noses, we were one runny nose short. No problem. The kid was here thirty seconds ago. Just look around and he'll show up in an instant. What can happen in thirty seconds?

We had recently heard of the following two incidents: In a nearby shopping center, a young mother with a child in a stroller was riding an elevator. When the doors of the elevator opened, there stood a man who reached down, snatched the little girl from the stroller, and took off running. Security services responded quickly and sealed off the shopping center. The child was found in a men's restroom. Her hair had been cut and dyed a different color, and she was dressed in boy's clothes.

In that same week, an acquaintance of ours had been shopping in a local discount store. Her small child was sitting in the shopping basket not more than a few feet from her. Out of the corner of her eye she watched as a woman in strange clothes reached down, scooped up the baby, and bolted for the door of the store. The mother's screams were rewarded. The baby snatcher was tackled and the baby saved. The culprit, however, shook loose and leaped out of the store and into a running car that was sitting just outside in anticipation of an instant getaway.

What can happen in thirty seconds? I tried to block these thoughts from my mind as I searched for my son. But as the seconds passed into minutes, any resolve I had to control my fears began to vanish in the crowd of humanity around me.

"Oh, God, where is my child?"

There are no words I know to describe my feelings at that time. If you are a parent and have been in a similar situation, I'm sure you will agree. There is a desperate terror that rises from deep within. Your heart literally pounds inside your chest. You couldn't spit if your life depended on it.

We split up. Someone covered the exit. Someone took this part of the park. Another adult took that part of the park. I found myself darting like an angry bee from one place to another in hopes of making some random connection with my lost child. I cannot honestly say how long I searched. Would you understand if I said it was an eternity? It was.

There I stood, out of breath and dripping sweat in the dead center of the park. My child was lost. What do you do now?

You pray like you've never prayed before—and I prayed that this lost child might somehow be found.

It has been years now since that night, but I can remember it in my mind as if it were happening right now. The sun was a pot of gold hanging on the horizon. It was hurling its last rays of daylight like spears across the land. The runways of the theme park emanated like spokes of a wheel from the center where I stood. As I looked down one of those spokes, a shaft of setting sunlight rested on the towhead of a small boy at the very end of the runway. All I could see was golden light reflecting off a golden head of hair.

Hope!

A part of me dared not run for fear that I'd get there too soon and find that my hope turned out to be a false one. But there is no way to stop your feet in that moment. They fly. As I got closer, the hope began to surge. The height was right and yes, the clothes were too. *It's true. Thank God it's true. It's my boy.*

There he stood, small hands in his small pockets, staring up at the merry-go-round, mesmerized by its music and enchantment.

"Oh! Hi, Daddy."

He didn't even know he was lost.No longer worried that some maniac might have been out to harm my child, I was ready to kill him myself.

The emotions at that time came flooding like water through a broken dam. There was relief and joy, anger and joy, frustration and joy, sudden weariness and joy. In the end it was the joy that dominated my soul. My child had been lost, and now he was found.

> What man among you, if he has a hundred sheep and has lost one of them, does not leave the ninety-nine in the open pasture, and go after the one which is lost, until he finds it? And when he has found it, he lays it on his shoulders, rejoicing. . . .
>
> Or what woman, if she has ten silver coins and loses one coin, does not light a lamp and sweep the house and search carefully until she finds it? And when she has found it, she calls together her friends and neighbors, saying, "Rejoice with me, for I have found the coin which I had lost!" In the same way, I tell you, there is joy in the presence of the angels of God over one sinner who repents. . . .
>
> The father said to his slaves, "Quickly bring out the best robe and put it on him, and put a ring on his hand and sandals on his feet; and bring the fattened calf, kill it, and let us eat and be merry; for this son of mine was dead, and has come to life again; he was lost, and has been found." And they began to be merry. (Luke 15:4-5, 8-10, 22-24)

For the first time in my life, I began to truly appreciate these teachings. I began to understand how God must feel about his lost children and the joy in heaven when one is found. I also better understand my role in helping to save the lost children of the world. What kind of person would ignore a friend's pleas to search for a lost child? Can I ignore God's pleas for help in finding his lost children?

My son, standing at the merry-go-round, is a good illustration of so many of the lost people of this world. Most of them don't have a clue that their heavenly Father is desperately seeking them. They stand mesmerized by the merry-go-rounds of life with their lights, music, and motion—all of which lead to an entertaining but meaningless existence.

I would not wish my experience on anyone. But God has been good to me. He has taught me a meaningful lesson.

CHAPTER 17

Nighttime Fevers

First . . . and last. These are, of course,
opposites. The concept of *first* is an absolute. First is first
and can never be otherwise. Your first date will always be
your first date. Your first job will always be your first job.
But the idea of *last* is a relative one, dependent upon
time. My "last job" when I was twenty-one years old will be
different from my "last job" when I'm sixty-five. Ask me
what was the last car I owned and my answer will depend
on when you ask me.

I think it is because of the absolute nature of *first* that
people tend to commemorate either formally or informally
many of the firsts in their lives. There was your first kiss. Do
you remember it? Mine wasn't a total disaster, but I certainly
wouldn't have won any awards for it. With my eyes squeezed
shut and my face a good twelve inches from hers, I went for
it like bobbing for a pea. I missed—a little bit high and a
good deal to the right of center. In fact, my technique was so

poor that I wound up marrying the girl five years later to redeem myself. She tells me I have improved somewhat.

Then there are all those firsts with our children: their first words, their first steps, their first day of school. These things seem to make such an impression on parents. I remember my son's first sneeze. He was newly born and only hours into this world. My wife, accompanied by a nurse, was holding him and proudly showing our son to his grandmothers. There was oohing and aahing and all of the delightful sounds that come from admiring grandparents. Then it happened. My son sneezed.

I couldn't believe it. No one else seemed to have noticed a thing. Then he did it again. I looked from one face to another in utter amazement as the doting continued without missing a beat. I was concerned and with good reason. After all, no one else in the room had been sneezing, but my newborn son had just done so, twice. As a brand-new father, I felt it was my responsibility to point out to the attending nurse that my son was in need of medical attention because he'd just sneezed.

I'll never forget the look she gave me. I knew instantly that I had just said the first foolish thing of my career as a parent. She assured me that children will do this from time to time and that sneezing was not at all abnormal. At that point I began to realize that this parenting thing was going to be trickier than I'd first thought.

The weeks passed by and my son did just fine. Being a new dad was great, and each day seemed to be graced by some new, delightful first. My first truly hard experience as a dad came somewhere in the middle of the night. It was my initial encounter with the nighttime fevers that can rage in a little one's body. I remember the fire in my son's cheek on mine as I held him, trying to rock him to health. Rocking

did nothing to relieve the fever but served well to absorb my
nervous energy of concern. I could feel the drumming of
his heart against my chest. I listened to the shallow and
rapid breaths that seemed to come only with great effort.
He was really too sick to cry but managed to squeeze out an
occasional pitiful whimper.

How does one describe the feeling of helplessness at those
times? I cannot. I could only hold this child and listen to the
squeaks of the rocker ticking off the nighttime hours. These
are good times to talk to the heavenly Father. I did. I told
him all those things that he already knew. This is the way
of prayer, for I have learned that prayer is mainly for my
benefit, and that there is comfort in telling God the things
he knows so well. I had questions as well. This was a new
suffering for me. My child was sick and knew pain. Why do
children have to suffer? Not just mine, but any child? Up to
this point in my life the question had been, for the most
part, theoretical. It had always been someone else's child.
I had grieved in these situations, but never as one who knew
what it meant to see your own child suffer.

I waited for God to respond but truly did not expect an
answer. For this was a question that had been posed throughout the ages, yet has remained unanswered. I asked this
question without any malice in my heart. But I asked simply
as a young, new father, confronted and confused by a fever
raging in my child's body.

How long did we talk? How long did I wait? Time is irregu-
lar in the deep night. It moves and pauses, drifts and floats.
But finally, I received my answer. It came from God's revelation in his Word, in just one word. That word was *Ishmael.*
Ishmael was the name given to Abraham's firstborn son. It
means "God hears." In my mind I sorted through Ishmael's
story. He knew suffering. As a child, he and his mother were

driven from Abraham's camp into the desert, with only a few of the necessities for survival. And when those gave out, the child suffered dearly.

> So Abraham rose early in the morning, and took bread and a skin of water, and gave them to Hagar, putting them on her shoulder, and gave her the boy, and sent her away. And she departed, and wandered about in the wilderness of Beersheba. And the water in the skin was used up, and she left the boy under one of the bushes. Then she went and sat down opposite him, about a bowshot away, for she said, "Do not let me see the boy die." And she sat opposite him, and lifted up her voice and wept. (Gen. 21:14-16)

Hagar did the last thing she could possibly do to give some measure of physical comfort to her son. She placed him under the shade of a bush. Just a bit of shade to protect Ishmael from the onslaught of the desert sun was the best she could do. Can you imagine the helplessness she felt? She could not, however, bear to watch the end. A bowshot's distance would be just enough to prevent her from hearing the cries of her child. The bush between her and Ishmael would serve to shield her eyes from watching death come like a thief to steal the life of her only child.

What grief could compare to that of watching your own child suffer from illness or from lack of food and water to the point of death? It is such an unnatural thing. Children are supposed to live to bury their parents—not the other way around.

Ishmael, "God hears," was the word that came to me that night as I held my child full of fever.

> And God heard the lad crying; and the angel of God
> called to Hagar from heaven, and said to her, "What is
> the matter with you, Hagar? Do not fear, for God has
> heard the voice of the lad where he is." (Gen. 21:17)

I received no answer that explained the suffering of innocent children. What I did receive was the assurance that children and parents alike are never alone in their suffering.
God hears the children crying wherever they are. He hears
the little children, and he hears the big children like me. I
also received the assurance that if my heart was breaking, so
was God's. For God is a father, and so am I. He knows the
pain of a father. In the simple word *Ishmael* I received a real
sense of comfort. The God of all creation really understood
this kind of hurt, and beyond that, he shared it with me. No
parent's heart will ever break alone. This heart pain will be
shared by God the Father.

Like Ishmael, my son recovered from his illness. Some
children do not. This I cannot explain. I can only offer the
word that ministered to me that night, with the prayer that it
may be used in some small way to minister to others as well.

CHAPTER 18

Who Really Spilled the Milk?

My wife is a nurse. It is a great profession, and she is a wonderful nurse. I consider myself to be one of those few men who is fortunate enough to be married to a woman who is great at two careers: being a mom and a professional. Nursing has the nice feature of being extremely flexible and allowing a person to work a wide range of hours. With small children, my wife could work only a couple of shifts in a two-week period, keep up her skills, and put some much appreciated bread on the table.

The greatest benefit in her working, however, is that I would have the opportunity of running the household for eight- to ten-hour stretches. I learned very quickly to appreciate my wife's abilities in this regard. So did my children. After having tried it myself, I began to be truly awestruck when I came home from my day at the office and found a nice dinner on the table, a picked-up house, and reasonably clean children. How did she do it?

One of the skills that I had to acquire was cooking. My only qualification in this regard was an eight-week stint of home economics in seventh grade, and half of that was taken up with sewing and learning how to iron a shirt. It is safe to conclude that I am no gourmet chef. But I am creative.

I discovered there are at least fifty ways to serve hot dogs. A favorite in our household was a tasty little dish that I called "Cheezie Weenie Bits." You take a hot dog and slice it up into little disks. Take a piece of American cheese and cut it into tiny little squares, placing one square on each bit of weenie. Bake it for whatever time you feel inspired and serve. Kids love it. It must be good, but I do not know from firsthand experience because I made it a rule never to eat my own cooking.

I can also make toast. If I feel daring, I will even make French toast.

French toast was the main entree for dinner one evening after my wife came home from a hard day of nursing. I admit that French toast is not a typical dinner entree for most families, but it is creative. French toast was one of the few things that I couldn't ruin, and even if I did, the good old sticky-sweet Log Cabin syrup could make anything palatable.

All that remained was to ask the blessing on the meal and go for it. Many families practice the fine art of passing food and conducting a meal in an orderly manner. We have strived to do the same, but with three small children, the task was sometimes beyond us. The children would eye the food offering, and if it was something they liked, they'd go for the biggest portion available. Of course the contrary was true when they disliked the menu. On this occasion, it was the former guideline that prevailed.

The three kids had scrutinized the platter in the center of the table and all sat coiled like springs ready to let fly at the word *Amen*. The word was pronounced and the attack launched. I didn't even have time to lift my head and open my eyes before I heard that distinctive sound of glass on glass and liquid cascading where it should not. With my head still bowed, I opened my eyes and saw a piece of French toast swimming on my plate in a lake of milk. My son, sitting next to me, had not accounted for my glass of milk in his attack on the food. His elbow had knocked my glass, sending it and its contents in my direction.

When I looked up I saw four sets of eyes staring at me in absolute silence, waiting for my response. The only expression I have a clear recollection of was that on the face of the offender. I remember big brown eyes the size of quarters. I remember a face full of anxiety and question.

My daughter, our youngest, was the first to break the silence.

"Na-na-na-naah-naah, Daddy spilled his mi-ilk!"

The oldest son was the next to speak. He chuckled and clucked, "Oh, Daddy spilled his milk!"

My wife even chimed in with an incredulous, "Honey, did you really spill your milk?"

That was the moment of truth. What would I say to my wife? Out of the corner of my eye, I could see the pain and the pleading in those brown eyes.

I hesitated but finally responded, "Oh well, I guess these things happen from time to time, don't they?" and I just laughed it off. The sigh of relief from the offender was, to me, both audible and visible. I replaced the soggy toast with a fresh piece on a clean plate and sat down ready to continue the meal in peace and tranquility.

No way!

This was just too great an opportunity for the family to pass up. After all, how often is it that Dad is the one to spill the milk? Spills during meals were unfortunately an all-too-common occurrence. But to have *Daddy* be the one to do it, *that* was real entertainment. And so for the rest of the meal, I was both subtly and overtly abused for being clumsy enough to spill my milk. It wasn't so bad when the kids teased me. What really got to me was every so often my wife would absentmindedly shake her head, smile, and mutter ever so audibly, "I can't believe you spilled your milk like that."

All during the meal I was doing a slow burn. This abuse was unjust and undeserved. I had hoped to simply take the rap and get on with things. It was not to be. Toward the end of the meal, the fuse had burned too long and too far. Dad was just about to blow. I even had the words all picked out and rehearsed in my mind.

"Look you all, let's just get one thing straight. I did not spill this glass of milk. It was this little klutz over here that did it, so lay off, OK?" And that was just for openers.

All I had to do was play out the scene in my mind to see that I was on the brink of doing something foolish and ugly, something that I knew I would regret the moment the words leaped from my lips. It took all the powers of restraint that I could muster, but I managed to keep my mouth shut.

After dinner, I retreated to the sink to wash the dishes and reflect on what had happened. I stood there contemplating how it was that I could let a little good-natured teasing upset me to the point that I would want to lash out in anger and hurt a son I loved with all my heart. I was ready to demean and castigate this child in front of the entire family for a simple act of knocking over the glass of milk.

Once again I became painfully aware of just how short I fall of the glory of God. What was it that made it so hard for me to cope with this teasing? I have concluded that there is within me a fundamental knee-jerk reaction against any perceived injustice against me. Whether it be a bad call in a sporting event, an unfair evaluation at work, or being accused of something I did not do, I react with feelings of anger against the injustice. I have enough trouble accepting criticism for my real faults and failings, let alone that which is without foundation. I wonder if I am so different from other people in this regard.

I can remember apologizing privately to my heavenly Father. And as I washed the remaining dishes, I could also feel the cleansing of spirit that comes with confession. This had been a messy meal.

> For while we were still helpless, at the right time Christ died for the ungodly. For one will hardly die for a righteous man; though perhaps for the good man someone would dare even to die. But God demonstrates His own love toward us, in that while we were yet sinners, Christ died for us. (Rom. 5:6-8)

> We beg you on behalf of Christ, be reconciled to God. He made Him who knew no sin to be sin on our behalf, that we might become the righteousness of God in Him. (2 Cor. 5:20-21)

> At that time two robbers were crucified with Him, one on the right and one on the left. And those passing by were hurling abuse at Him, wagging their heads. (Matt. 27:38-39)

> Have this attitude in yourselves which was also in Christ Jesus, who, although He existed in the form of

God, did not regard equality with God a thing to be
grasped, but emptied Himself, taking the form of a
bond-servant, and being made in the likeness of men.
And being found in appearance as a man, He humbled Himself by becoming obedient to the point of
death, even death on a cross. (Phil. 2:5-8)

The truth of these Scriptures began to pulse and radiate
deep inside my heart as I reflected on that meal. I had willingly taken the blame and abuse for my son's action. It was a
trivial thing that I did because I loved him. But it took every
last ounce of willpower that I had to do it, and even so, I
struggled with the injustice of it. But to think, Christ loved
me so much that he willingly and perfectly took the blame
for my sin and the sin of all mankind! What a wondrous display of the love God has for us.

In the end, two things became much clearer to me as a
result of that spilled glass of milk. The first was that my
own righteousness is such a fragile and unreliable thing.
I am utterly dependent on God's Spirit to mold me into a
Christlike person. The second and even better thing was a
renewed sense of God's love for me, a sinner. What better
evidence could I want? At the Day of Judgment, when the
works of unrighteousness must all be accounted for, I'll
need only look to Christ. He has accounted for mine.

CHAPTER 19

Woo-woos in the Night

I have to confess that I have an irrational fear. It's no secret to my friends and family. I am afraid of . . . butter. There, now all the world knows. I truly am afraid of butter and anything that looks, smells, or tastes like butter. I won't get near the stuff. Cheese, sour cream, and mayonnaise are all in the same category. It's not merely that I don't *like* it—I truly am *afraid* of eating it. When I was a little kid, I ate an entire stick of butter at one time, and it made me so sick that whenever I think of the stuff, I want to gag.

So I live a life without butter, cheese, sour cream, or anything else that might be like them. I don't even like them when they're disguised in something else. For example, people are always putting sour cream or cream cheese in Jell-O. This disturbs me greatly. So I have a rule about Jell-O: Don't eat any Jell-O that you can't see through.

I freely admit that my fear of butter is totally irrational. Irrational fears are hard for other people to cope with.

I have noticed that, as a father, I have two ways of reacting to my children's fears. When their fears are rational, my natural reaction is all that it should be. I feel very empathetic, and I want to do everything I can to bring peace to their troubled hearts. But when their fears are irrational, I tend to feel frustrated and impatient.

On one occasion somewhere between midnight and dawn, my sleep was assaulted by a terrified boy doing a frantic little dance by my bed and screaming at me. It was clear to me that he had been badly frightened by something, but he wasn't fully awake.

I got out of bed, held the boy by the shoulders, and tried to wake him in hopes that it would dispel the fear and bring some comfort to him. No good; he would not wake up. I pulled out the trusty old comforter and pillow that we kept for such occasions and laid the boy down next to my bed. This was a tried-and-tested remedy, so when I myself rolled back into bed, I did so with a good deal of optimism that I would soon be resuming my own quiet repose.

No such luck. It was as if my son was rigged with some sort of giant mousetrap-like spring. He would lie quietly on his back for several moments, and then he'd sit bolt upright and start crying. Since he was lying right next to my bed, I would mechanically reach out with my arm and push the little guy back to a prone position as I muttered some words of encouragement. Up, down, . . . mutter, mutter, mutter. . . . Up, down, . . . mutter, mutter, mutter. . . . Up, down, . . . mutter, mutter, mutter. This went on for some time until I realized that the tried-and-tested remedy wasn't going to work.

I changed my tactic. I took my own pillow, grabbed a blanket, and flopped down on the floor next to my son. It didn't help. Even though I was right next to the child, he would not stop his whimpering.

In my mind, there was absolutely no reason for my son to be afraid. After all, there I was, lying on the floor right next to him. He had to at least understand that he wasn't alone and there was nothing to be afraid of.

My daughter's fear of Woo-woos, on the other hand, was completely rational. It all started one night when she came running into my room, fleeing some imagined monster. I threw off the covers, scooped her up in my arms, and tried to squeeze the fear from her trembling little body.

"Honey, what's wrong?"

"It's after me, Daddy, it's after me!"

"What's after you, honey?"

"I don't know, but it's after me."

This was not going to be easy. *How am I supposed to protect this kid from whatever it is when I don't know what it is?*

"Well, what does it look like?"

"I don't know."

"Is it big or little?"

"I don't know."

"Well, can you go back to bed now?"

"Oh no, Daddy. It's after me, and it's just outside my room. I know it is! Oh, Daddy, I can't go back to my room."

This was just great. *I don't know what it is. I don't know even if it's big or little. All I know is that it's after my daughter.*

"Well, honey, how do you know it's after you if you don't know what it looks like?"

"Because I heard it, Daddy."

"You heard it? What did it say?"

"I don't know, Daddy."

"But I thought you said you heard it?"

"I did hear it, Daddy; I did!"

"Well, what did it sound like?"

"Oh, Daddy! It went *wooooooooo-wwwwwwwwwwooooooooooooo*, and it's after me, I just know it!"

This was progress. At least now I knew what it sounded like. It was something outside my little girl's room that went *woo-woooo*. All I had to do was investigate, and sure enough, a simple explanation was found. It turned out to be nothing more than the wind blowing through an open window down at the end of the hall. My daughter refused to be consoled by this explanation. The result was that I forfeited an additional amount of my sleep until my little girl could find hers.

For some days after that fearful episode, our family had to keep a sharp eye out for "Woo-woos" that might be lurking around the house. Fortunately for the well-being of both my daughter and myself, the Woo-woos kept their distance. It also helped to keep the window closed at night.

I thought that we had seen (or should I say heard) the last of the Woo-woos, when my daughter came screaming into the living room late one evening just before bedtime. She was almost inconsolable. She was convinced that there was a Woo-woo under her bed and that it was after her. It took some time to calm her down, and when I did, I assured her there wasn't a Woo-woo under her bed but that I would go and look anyway. I invited her to go with me. She declined.

On the way into the bedroom, I wondered to myself what good this little exercise in Woo-woo snooping was going to do. I would look under the bed, there would be nothing there, and my daughter would believe it was hiding somewhere else. This had the makings of a short night of sleep. Even as I got down on my hands and knees in her bedroom to search for this Woo-woo, I was already planning my strategy for dealing with coming up blank. I dutifully lifted the bed skirt, expecting to see nothing . . . and there was my son with a wicked smile on his face. I'd caught myself a real live Woo-woo.

Apparently my son had been enjoying the Woo-woo alert of the last several days and took it upon himself to add a little extra anxiety to his sister's life. To that end, he had hidden himself under her bed and grabbed her ankles as she was getting into it. Mission accomplished!

And so my daughter's fear was very justified. There were weird noises in the night that went *woo-woo*. And then there were these little hands under her bed that grabbed at her.

Reflecting on my children's nighttime fears brought back the memory of one night when, as a little boy, I was wakened in the middle of the night by a terrible thunderstorm. It came rumbling and flashing through the night. I remember a sudden burst of lightning and thunder right outside my window. The brilliant light stabbed my eyes and left me with visions of horrible faces lurking wherever I turned my head. The terror took my breath away and turned my skin cold and clammy.

It was my father who came to my rescue. It was the strength of his arm around me that warded off the fear of those nighttime intruders. I can remember lying awake, watching those things continue to float around the room, long after my dad had fallen asleep with his arm still draped over my shoulder. I can remember even taunting one of those things.

"I'm not scared of you. You can do anything you want and I don't care. My dad's here!" As long as my dad was there, I had no reason to fear.

It was this recollection of a night years past that made me see my own children's situation in a different light. You don't deal with nighttime fears—whether rational or irrational—with explanations. You just reach out and put your arm around the child.

I remember what it was like to fear the night. And because I have known this fear, I am able to comfort my children. For this, there is a spiritual parallel.

> We all know he did not come as an angel but as a human being. . . . For since he himself has now been through suffering and temptation, he knows what it is like when we suffer and are tempted, and he is wonderfully able to help us. (Heb. 2:16, 18, TLB)

My children are occasionally surprised when I tell a story from my childhood days. They have trouble thinking of me as ever being anything but a dad because that is the only way they have ever related to me. A similar thing can happen to us with God. If we become accustomed to relating to him most often as the heavenly Father, we tend to overlook the fact that Christ was indeed just like us. He knows exactly what life on earth is all about. He has lived here. He has suffered here. He has cried here. He even died here. He knows.

And because he knows, he can comfort and help us in unique and perfect ways. It is good to remind ourselves of this fact. It isn't anything new; it's just important to remember.

CHAPTER 20

Who Is This at My Back Door?

Have you ever watched a young child near a puddle of water? Puddles attract little feet just like a magnet attracts paper clips. It's a great thing to watch when it isn't your kid. There it is, a puddle just waiting there on a sidewalk for some little kid. Then the kid appears and spots the puddle out of the corner of his eye. He walks up to it like he hasn't seen it. There is a moment of slight hesitation, then the child inevitably takes that deliberate, inquisitive step into the water. The first tentative step is usually followed by a second confident splash.

What happens next depends on the proximity of the parent. If there's a parent near, there comes at this point a quick and decisive reprimand. If, however, no parent is around to observe this behavior, the child can continue playing in the water to his or her heart's delight, without the slightest thought of the effect of puddles on shoes, socks, or any other article of clothing.

Puddles are by no means the only thing that has this effect on kids. Mud, sand, and dirt in general often provoke very similar behavior. I have observed that many kids don't care in the least if, as a consequence of their actions, they get unbelievably dirty. Kids will even *eat* a certain amount of dirt and sand, as long as you don't serve it to them on a plate and tell them it's good for them. If they have any aversion at all to getting dirty, it seems to be outweighed by their basic curiosity about the texture, form, and general physical properties of a mysterious substance. It's not enough to just look at something. Kids want to touch, smell, and taste it. They are driven to employ all of their sensory powers in the exploration of their world.

My wife and I have had many such experiences with our kids. Two seem to stand out in particular. My wife knew it was going to be bad when our very young son came in from playing and said to her, "You'll never believe what he's done now!" He was speaking of his even younger brother, who had been playing harmlessly in the backyard sandbox. For some reason, this small boy had the inspiration to get a large bottle of Hershey's chocolate syrup and use it to make things in the sandbox. Chocolate syrup on a hot summer afternoon has amazing binding properties. The sandbox had been transformed into one large mass of sticky chocolate sand cookie. Our son was most proud of his creation. His mother was not pleased.

It wasn't long after that incident that my wife responded to a knock at the back door and was greeted by an alien life-form. Standing at the back door was an unidentifiable creature about forty inches tall. It had the shape of a small human, but other than that, it was like nothing she had ever seen before. It was covered with a uniform layer of chalky white stuff from tip to toe. When it moved, it emitted small

puffs of this fine powderlike substance, leaving a trail of
white dust wherever it went.

For a few moments, the confrontation between my wife
and this thing was a silent one, due primarily to my wife's
shock. Finally, it spoke.

"Hi, Mommy!"

*It couldn't be. This thing couldn't possibly be a child of mine.
After all, my children were all cleaned up and dressed in good
clothes before they went out. What is this thing calling me Mommy?*

Every household has certain chores that just don't seem
to get done as often as they should. One of these chores at
our house has been cleaning out the ashes in the Weber
grill. I had evidently procrastinated too long on this particular task, and now my son had taken the liberty to do it for
me. Actually, I don't believe my son had the slightest inten-
tion of doing me any favors. He had just been exploring in
the garage and had come upon this mysterious substance in
the ash pan of our grill. Intrigued by this discovery, he went
on to see what else was inside the grill. Some disassembly of
the grill was apparently required to satisfy the full measure
of his curiosity, and in the process, he managed not only to
totally cover himself with a layer of fine white ash, but also to
blanket the entire garage and its contents with the same
insoluble substance. It was as if he had gotten ahold of an
industrial vacuum machine, put it on reverse, and blown the
ashes throughout the garage.

And now here he was, standing at the back door, waiting
to be warmly received by the mother he loved.

No way!

I believe what happened next was the result of one of
those flashes of brilliance that come to parents when confronted with the extraordinaries of parental life. After the
initial shock had subsided, my wife took full appraisal of the

situation and concluded, quite correctly, that what stood before her *was* one of her offspring and that this little boy was in need of some serious cleaning to restore him to a proper state of hygiene. There was, however, one problem. There was no way she was going to let this kid cross the door-step of her house in that condition. If there was cleaning to be done, it had to be done outside.

A quick survey of the backyard provided a ready solution to the dilemma. There was the garden hose, all attached and ready to go. The fact that garden hoses only spray cold water was inconsequential in my wife's estimation. My son was of a very different opinion, but that didn't matter. So off came every last stitch of clothing, and on went the cold spray from the hose. Ashes don't dissolve in water, so a hard spray of water was needed to remove the film of ash from the boy.

The remedy accomplished its intended result. In the end, the boy was restored to his normal color and was, in fact, quite clean. A secondary result was also achieved: My son learned that getting dirty can have painful consequences— if you have a mother who wants clean kids. Getting sprayed with freezing water was not pleasant, but it was necessary to get him clean.

Sin in the lives of God's children is a lot like this example. Sin is spiritual dirt. In fact, people often use the expression "feeling dirty" to describe their feelings of guilt from sin. Conversion brings, among other things, the forgiveness of sins, and so we speak and sing of having our sins "washed away."

> Wash yourselves, make yourselves clean; remove the evil of your deeds from My sight. (Isa. 1:16)

This cleansing involved a most painful process, and we should not take it lightly. It required the bloody crucifixion of Christ to bring about the cleansing of God's children. When Christ endured the pain of the Cross, no one understood in the least what was actually going on before their eyes—that God was cleaning up a world full of dirty sin. (My son, on the other hand, did not suffer quietly. Anyone in the neighborhood could have easily understood what was happening when they saw—and heard—him standing in front of that cold, hard stream of water!)

In addition, the process of making us more like Christ is one of continual cleansing of sin from our lives, which can also be a painful process. Just as a mother who wants clean children will use a cold spray of water to get the job done, God can use pain to purge from us our sinful patterns of living. Sometimes God will use pain in our lives to refine us and to make us more pure.

I have found these thoughts to be an encouragement, and yet I find myself reminded that sin is a serious business and I ought not to take God's grace for granted. Cleansing from sin had much too high a price for us to do so.

> He was pierced through for our transgressions, He was crushed for our iniquities; the chastening for our well-being fell upon Him, and by His scourging we are healed. (Isa. 53:5)

CHAPTER 21

Dead Bunnies Make
Bad Show-and-Tell

I came home from work one spring evening and was greeted with an unusual amount of excitement. That afternoon, my children had found a little bunny rabbit, which they were certain had been abandoned by its mother. I went out to see this discovery, and sure enough, there it was, a small and rather frail-looking ball of fur with long pink ears.

I suggested that we had better let it alone, feeling confident that the mother would come to its aid. The children in chorus assured me that they had been looking for the mother all afternoon and there was absolutely no chance of her returning. I, however, insisted that we leave it alone at least until after dinner. In spite of the protests, that is exactly what we did. Later that evening we cautiously returned to find the bunny in the exact same spot. It had not moved in the least. It became apparent to me that this little guy was truly abandoned, suffering, and in some distress. I agreed that we could take it in and try to nurse it back to health.

We immediately set out to fashion some sort of bunny recovery plan. The kids got an old box and made what they thought would serve as a suitable bunny hutch. They rigged the box with a light bulb for warmth and lined it with grasses, soft cloth, and whatever else they could find that they thought a bunny might like. My wife enthusiastically joined the effort. A critical care nurse by profession, she has an instinctive compassion for anything that is sick. She warmed up some milk and proceeded to feed the bunny with an eye dropper.

I supervised. Privately, I was worried where all this might lead. Should this work out and the bunny indeed recover, I was fearful that I would, by default, become the legal guardian of a pet bunny. The thought did not appeal to me.

The bunny went to sleep that night in the boys' bedroom. My sleep went undisturbed throughout the night, but morning came early and with alarm. My younger son came running into the bedroom and burst on the scene like a closet full of falling pots and pans. In the fog of those semi-wakeful moments, I was totally unable to comprehend what this child was doing or saying. I sat there on the edge of my bed and tried to figure out who I was, where I was, and why this child was banging a stuffed rabbit on my nightstand.

That little rabbit sure looked real.

Then it all started to come back to me. The mist was rising. The bunny *was* real . . . real dead and real stiff.

"Look, Dad. I think something's very wrong with our bunny. He's not moving at all. He won't answer to his name, and look, Dad, he's stiff like a board!"

My son kept rapping that poor little stiff bunny on my nightstand.

"Please don't do that anymore!" I took the bunny and got up to face the rest of the day.

You can probably imagine most of what transpired the rest of that morning. There were some tears and grieving at the loss of our little friend. Children have the ability to bond so quickly to objects of their affection that it was hard to let go. They wanted to keep the bunny. I explained as best as I could that this wasn't possible.

"But can't I at least bring him to school for show-and-tell? Nobody has ever brought anything as awesome as a stiff bunny to show-and-tell before. Can't I, Dad? Oh please, can't I?"

I thought for a moment and asked, "Well, when do you have show-and-tell? Is it this morning or is it in the afternoon?"

My wife instantly shot me one of those looks that let me know she had begun to doubt my sanity. I wasn't really going to allow our son to take a dead bunny for show-and-tell, was I?

Actually, up until that moment I had been considering it, because my son did have a good point. Bringing a stiff little bunny to show-and-tell would make for a significant and memorable experience. But a few more moments of thought and another look or two from my wife convinced me that this would not be good for me *or* my son's class that day.

"No, Son. I'm afraid you can't bring Bunny to show-and-tell today."

My wife gave a sigh of relief, but my son was not as content with my decision. He accepted it, however, and with his shoulders slumped with the burdens of that morning, he turned and walked away, no bunny, no pet, and no show-and-tell.

I watched him slowly walk away, dragging his feet as if

LESSONS ABOUT GOD

there were weights on his ankles. My heart was pained with
each step. It hurts to see your children hurt.

That afternoon we held a funeral for our bunny and buried him in the backyard under the shade of a lilac bush. Later
that evening at bedtime, the kids wanted to talk about the
bunny. No doubt you already know what they wanted to know.

"Daddy, do bunnies go to heaven?"

It is a question that has been asked thousands, if not mil-
lions, of times before, not necessarily about bunnies, but
about dogs, cats, birds, hamsters, or any other animal that
has filled the precious role of a pet.

There may well be animal life in heaven, but animals on
earth do not have souls. Their physical death on earth is
final—and this truth is of no comfort to a child. It can, however, serve a useful purpose in that it stands in stark contrast
to the hope that we, as Christians, have of an eternal life
with God where all things will be made perfect; a life where
there is no longer the sting of death nor the pain that comes
with living in a fallen world.

This hope and assurance is of great comfort to children.
It wasn't long after that I was studying Numbers 20, where
Moses and his brother Aaron take that one last long walk
together to the top of Mount Hor. It was there that Aaron
would die.

> Then the Lord spoke to Moses and Aaron at Mount
> Hor by the border of the land of Edom, saying, "Aaron
> shall be gathered to his people; for he shall not enter
> the land which I have given to the sons of Israel,
> because you rebelled against My command at the
> waters of Meribah. Take Aaron and his son Eleazar,
> and bring them up to Mount Hor; and strip Aaron of
> his garments and put them on his son Eleazar. So

Aaron will be gathered to his people, and will die there." (Num. 20:23-26)

Of all the things God asked of Moses, I believe this command was as difficult as anything for him to carry out. For the last forty years, Aaron had served with him to help lead the people of Israel in the wilderness. They had gone through so much together, and now from this point on, Moses would have to do it without the help of his brother, his priest, and his friend.

As I studied these verses I was struck with the phrase *gathered to his people*. It struck me as odd because Aaron's people were about to enter the Promised Land. I thought he was *leaving* his people. But the more I thought about it, the more the phrase seemed to perfectly depict the real truth of death for children of God. God's children belong with him. Death indeed represents the gathering up of God's children to be with their people. The hope that we have as the family of God is that we will live together, forever, in the presence of God.

Several weeks after we buried the bunny, the kids decided that they wanted to dig him up and see if he was still there. Fortunately, they came to me first to ask permission. I, of course, told them no. But the incident served to remind me how important this issue was with the children. They needed to know the hope of eternal life.

I suspect that grown-ups need to know this hope every bit as much as kids do. But adults so often have lost, at least outwardly, their childlike sensitivity to spiritual longings. We may not be aware of our need or be able to act on it as easily as the kids' desire to dig up their bunny, but it is there nonetheless. Our family's incident with the bunny has encouraged me to be more faithful in sharing this certain hope that is available to anyone who will accept the salvation offered by Jesus Christ.

CHAPTER 22

Treasure in the Tower

Parenthood has brought with it all sorts of challenges. Some of them I expected. Others I did not. One of the significant unexpected challenges that I have faced as a parent is that of the Birthday Party.

When I was growing up, birthday parties were no big deal. You went to the kid's house, played "pin the tail on the donkey" and other such games, had cake and ice cream, opened presents, and went home. If, perchance, it was one of the more rowdy types of parties, you might have a spanking-machine line or play the game where you stamp on balloons tied to the other kids' feet. But other than that, things were pretty tame.

These days, there has been an escalation in kids' expectations of what a birthday party is all about. This generally translates into big bucks. My own kids have gone to some pretty elaborate and expensive birthday parties. I am glad that they have been able to enjoy these experiences, but I have been quite reluctant to attempt to duplicate them. We are not a poor family by any standard, but we aren't really wealthy. So how do you throw a good birthday party that shows your kids how much you appreciate them without having to get a second mortgage on the house?

This problem was particularly acute when my son hit twelve years of age. Let's face it. Twelve-year-old birthday parties are tough. But my wife and I took on the challenge and, at the outset, committed ourselves to the principle that we weren't just going to go to some extravagant "Birthday Palace" and drop a lot of bucks. We wanted to find a way, other than spending a lot of money, to show our appreciation to our son.

At this age, kids like a good mystery. So we decided to have a find-your-own-party party. It started at our house with an after-school snack of birthday cupcakes and milk. Inside each cupcake was a puzzle piece that, when fit together with every other kid's piece, provided a clue of where to go next. I went about twenty minutes ahead of the kids and left clues telling them where to go next. I left a clue at the local popcorn and candy shop that sent them on to find a clue at a convenience store that sent them on to somewhere else. At each spot, I would buy in advance for each of the kids a small bag of popcorn, a soft drink, or some other modest confectionery. The merchants were all very pleased to cooperate and would insist that the kids sing a rousing rendition of "Happy Birthday" before they would turn over the next clue. I even left a clue at the local library on page 12 of the book *Treasure Island*.

The hunt ended at the college where I teach. My office is located in a building that is more than 150 years old. At the top of this building is an old bell tower. The kids had picked up along the way an "old" map that allegedly showed the way to the "tower treasure." I had drawn it out myself and had given it an aged appearance by singeing it with a match. The school's security department had agreed to unlock the tower for a short specified period of time, during which the kids found their way up an old and very mysterious staircase that led to the tower.

Upon reaching the tower, the kids did indeed find a treasure chest, which was full of twelve-year-old-boy treasure. I had stumbled on a toy and novelty shop that was going out of business and selling everything for fifteen cents on the dollar. For about twenty bucks, I managed to literally fill a chest with baseball cards, little magic tricks, books, whistles, and other sorts of items. To the boys, this was indeed a treasure worth its weight in yo-yos. The guys had a great time sorting it all out and finding, to their great delight, that there was one of each item for every boy in the group.

The party was a hit, and we managed to pull it off for around thirty dollars. We have since done the same sort of thing with my other son. For that party, we gave the children inexpensive but functional compasses and had them use the compasses to guide them around a park to find clues to lead them on their search. This time the treasure at the end was a bag full of the kids' towels and swimming suits, which we had surreptitiously acquired earlier in the day. At the end of the hunt came a swim at the pool.

These turned out to be fun parties for our family. The kids enjoyed them, and the parties were memorable for the birthday children. It was especially fun to watch how all the pieces of the puzzle, all the clues, fit together to lead the kids to the end of their hunt. All they knew was enough to get them to the next step.

This is a good illustration of how the heavenly Father reveals his will for our lives. We seldom, if ever, know more than we need to get to the next step of life. At just the right time and place, he lets us know where to go and what to do next.

> Make me know Thy ways, O Lord; teach me Thy paths. Lead me in Thy truth and teach me, for Thou art the God of my salvation; for Thee I wait all the day. (Ps. 25:4-5)

I would rather know in advance the whole route from start to finish, but that isn't the way God works. If the kids at the birthday party had known the whole mystery from the beginning, I daresay there would have been no joy in pursuing the clues.

Our ignorance about the destiny of our lives forces us to put our trust in God, believing that he will lead us to what will ultimately be for our great benefit. The treasure we seek is not in some ancient tower, but rather in heaven. There can therefore be joy in the hunt, for each day of our lives brings us closer to our eternal reward.

Knowing that God has indeed planned for us a life full of discovery can add joy and confidence to our existence. It also gives us reason to be more patient in our living because we know that God will complete his perfect will for us in his time.

> "For I know the plans that I have for you," declares the Lord, "plans for welfare and not for calamity to give you a future and a hope." (Jer. 29:11)

CHAPTER 23

Whispers in the Night

I learned very early in my career as a parent that it was a mistake to look at the clock when the kids woke me in the middle of the night. Looking at the clock somehow engages a greater portion of my consciousness and arouses emotions that otherwise lay dormant in my sleepy state. All it takes is one glance, and . . . *Oh no! It's 2:30.* The digital numbers on the bedside clock glare at you and dare you to try to get back to sleep.

"I will sleep, I will sleep, I will sleep!"

At least that is what I tell myself, but it's no use. I am awake, angry, and frustrated because it's 2:30 in the morning, when reasonable humans are sleeping. And here I am with this very unreasonable little person who doesn't understand train schedules, commuting, rush hour, meetings, and the daily demands of putting bread on the table. No, it is much better not to look at the clock. If I don't know the time, I can always lie to myself and believe that dawn is still far away and sweet repose yet waits for me 'neath the down feather quilt of my bed.

So it was that night. From the depths of my slumber I was being summoned by the faintest of whispers in my ear.

"Daddy . . . Daaaaaady . . . Daaaaaaaaaaaaaaaady . . ."

It was, of course, my son. He was of preschool age and prone to getting up in the middle of the night for all of the normal sorts of reasons that children his age can conjure up. Steven was quiet by nature, and even his nocturnal prowlings tended to be hushed. He would shuffle into our room and rouse me with breathy whispers in my ear.

This night stands out in my memory because I remember being particularly annoyed by that confounded whispering.

"Daaaaaaaady."

"What do you want, Steven?"

"Can I sleep on your floor?"

This may sound like an unusual request, but for Steven it was normal. He liked to sleep on the carpeted floor in our bedroom. I figured out why one night when I tried it myself. The furnace in our home was beneath our bedroom. Just like a puppy, Steven would curl up over the heating ducts that ran beneath the flooring. The vibrations from the furnace fan and the heat coursing through the ductwork were very soothing. The combination of hum and heat had a way of lulling you to sleep.

There was a period when my wife and I vigorously resisted these nocturnal intrusions. We tried all the standard defenses, including a "spanking spoon" that was placed strategically at the door of my son's room to reinforce the consequences of crossing the nighttime boundaries. But when he would still come to us, carrying the spoon, all too willing to pay the price for crossing the mark, I decided that the experts were nuts. If my kid wanted to see me in the middle of the night it was no crime.

Deciding that it was no crime is not, however, the same as saying that I welcomed him with wild enthusiasm. I sort of feel the same way about being wakened in the middle of the night as I do about catching a cold. A cold now and then is inevitable, and you just try to get through it and minimize the symptomatic unpleasantries.

"Yes, Steven, you can sleep on my floor."

Quickly, I rolled over and slipped back into an unconscious state.

"Daddy . . . Daaaaady . . . Daaaaaaaaaaaady!"

Oh, no! Not again! Please don't let it be. I'm not really hearing this, am I?

"Daaaaaaaady!"

"What, Steven?" The words were slurred.

"I don't have my blanket."

His complaint, I guess, was a reasonable one. Even Linus has to have his blanket. After all, Steven's was handmade for him by his great-grandmother, every stitch made with love and all that. *All right, I'll get it for him.* This was, however, a dangerous venture. It required getting up and maneuvering about the house in the dark. Turning on the lights was too risky—I might wake up. If I could keep the lights off, maybe I'd just think it was all a dream. Then I could fall asleep again as soon as my head reached the pillow.

Mechanically, I plodded to Steven's room and retrieved the blanket. Reversed. Retracing my steps, I successfully negotiated my way back to my bedroom. I flipped the blanket over my son and slid into bed. There was a moment or two when my mind flickered with the stimulation of the last moments. But quickly any spark of consciousness was snuffed out by the deep desire for sleep. I smiled as sleep came.

"Daddy . . . Daaaaaaady!"

Any sign of a smile dissipated. I was plagued with a sudden fear that I might once again have heard myself being called.

"Daaaaaaaady!"

That which I feared . . . you know the rest. For whatever was sure to follow, I doubted that I would have much patience.

"Daddy, the blanket is the wrong way."

You see, Steven's blanket was made with stripes down its length. I had laid it down with the stripes across Steven's body, and as a result, his feet were uncovered. There was an instant tension within me. *Why doesn't he just curl up with his feet under the blanket?*

"Daaaaady!"

I decided it was no use. I don't like cold feet either. I slid the covers off and slowly rolled out of bed. I told myself, *Don't think; just straighten out the blanket and get back to bed.* With my eyes closed, I bent down and rearranged the blanket. Steven's feet were now covered.

"OK, Steven, are you warm enough?"

"Yes, Daddy."

"Is everything fine?"

"Yes, Daddy."

"Are you sure there's nothing else you want?"

"Yes, Daddy."

Good. I could now crawl back into bed, secure in the knowledge that there was no further reason to have to get up again. That knowledge was enough to put my troubled spirit back at rest. And so, I dozed off into that mindless world of sleep.

"Daaaddy . . . Daaaaddy . . . Daaaaaaaddy."
IT CAN'T BE! I'M NOT HEARING THIS!

A slow burn started somewhere in the pit of my stomach and flowed throughout the rest of my being. Maybe you too have experienced the unadulterated feeling of raw anger. *This is the last straw! He told me I could go back to sleep! This isn't fair!* I mumbled out loud, "What does this child want now!"

"Daddy, I'm thirsty. Can I have a drink of water?"

I tried to respond, but fortunately the anger I felt choked the words that instinctively came to mind. So I just lay there and steamed.

"Daddy, please can I have some water?"

I was fully awake. I was suddenly aware of everything around me. I knew I would never sleep again. The anger subsided somewhat as I grieved over the night's rest that was lost.

"Daddy!"

What should I say to this little sleep robber?

Now, it doesn't always happen this way. It doesn't even happen a majority of the time. But once in a while, in these late-night moments when the forces of childhood confront the forces of parenthood, the Spirit of God touches my mind and directs my thought to some seed of his Word that was planted there long before. This time, the verses from Matthew 7:9-11 suddenly sprouted.

> What man is there among you, when his son shall ask him for a loaf, will give him a stone? Or if he shall ask for a fish, he will not give him a snake, will he? If you then, being evil, know how to give good gifts to your children, how much more shall your Father who is in heaven give what is good to those who ask Him!

My dialogue with God went something like this:

"Now Lord, do you mean to tell me that my son's relationship with me has something to do with his understanding of our relationship with you, our heavenly Father?"

Yes.

"Do you mean that if I bother to get up and get this glass of water, it just might help him understand something of your love and sacrifice for us?"

Yes.

"I very much doubt it, but I'm really too tired to argue."

I got up and grudgingly got the water. I was half tempted to throw it at the boy, but squelched the impulse.

"OK, you've got your water, right?"

"Yes, Daddy."

"You've got your blanket, right?"

"Yes, Daddy."

"There's nothing else that you can possibly want, is there?"

"No, Daddy."

"Can I go back to sleep now?"

"Yes, Daddy."

Flop! I'm back in bed.

Sleep would not come. The house creaked and groaned its night sounds. The sound of a west-bound freight train mumbled its way through the darkness. Turn this way. Turn that way. Sleep would not come.

"Daaaady . . ."

NO! NO! NO! This isn't happening. He promised me there was nothing else.

I gritted my teeth and hissed, "What *now?*"

"I love you, Daddy."

Those four little words, "I love you, Daddy," are the most precious words a father can hear. These were the words spoken by a child to a father in appreciation for a glass of water in the night.

The water was given begrudgingly. My heavenly Father gives freely.

I had given because it was my duty. I have received out of the abundance of the Father's love.

The water was so little. My Father in heaven has given so much.

And yet for this simple glass of water, my child responded with thanksgiving and love. When was the last time my heavenly Father heard *his* child's sincere expression of love?

I thought one more time about those four whispered words that came floating up in the night. I could only respond, "Thank you, God. I love you!" And with that, Steven and I drifted peacefully off to sleep.

Find Encouragement for Parenting with Tyndale House Books

FAMILY TRADITIONS THAT LAST A LIFETIME
Karen M. Ball and Karen L. Tornberg   0-8423-1371-0
This collection of traditions from families nationwide will help
you create meaningful, lasting family bonds.

PARENTING PASSAGES *(New! Fall 1994)*
Dave Veerman   0-8423-5038-1
The author draws on interviews and personal experience to
lead parents through the joys and traumas of each stage of the
parenting process.
Available on Tyndale Living Audio   0-8423-7432-9

QUICK TO LISTEN, SLOW TO SPEAK
Robert E. Fisher   0-8423-5111-6
Learn to express love to family members through listening skills,
constructive criticism, and disagreements rather than arguments.

SINGLE PARENTING
Robert G. Barnes, Jr.   0-8423-5920-6
With biblical, in-depth answers to important questions single
parents have, the author points the way to personal and
family healing.

WAIT QUIETLY *(New! Fall 1994)*
Dean Merrill 0-8423-7917-7
Busy parents will find scriptural encouragement in these Bible
passages, meditations, memory verses for kids, and space for
written reflections.